Praise for *Toxic Men*

"Dr. Lillian Glass is a gift to all women who want to learn how to make smart choices for themselves, especially when it comes to men."
—Dr. Robi Ludwig, renowned media psychologist

"With partner abuse and domestic on the rise, Dr. Lilllian Glass's new book, *Toxic Men*, is a must for women thinking about getting into relationships or already involved with males who exhibit controlling behaviors. This book could save your life and your self-esteem by teaching what you need to know about men who stay frogs even after you kiss them."
—Criminal profiler Pat Brown, author of *The Profiler:*
My Life Hunting Serial Killers and Psychopaths

"As a criminal defense attorney, I have been involved in representing many cases involving domestic violence. That is why I can recommend that every woman read this book. Dr. Glass has done a great service in educating women how to identify toxic relationships and what to do if you are involved in such a relationship."
—Michael "Mickey" Sherman, renowned criminal defense attorney and legal analyst for *CBS News* and regular commentator on numerous television shows and networks, including *Nancy Grace*, MSNBC, CNBC,

D1470489

TOXIC MEN

10 Ways to Identify, Deal with, and
Heal from the Men Who Make Your
Life Miserable

Lillian Glass, PhD
BESTSELLING AUTHOR OF *Toxic People*™

Avon, Massachusetts

Dedication

‿⁓

To anyone who has shed a tear or suffered a broken heart, broken bone, or broken spirit as the result of a Toxic Man. Your voice has been heard. You will never be silenced again! Through these pages, may you be enlightened and empowered forever. ~ Dr. Lillian Glass

Published by
Adams Media, a division of F+W Media, Inc.
57 Littlefield Street, Avon, MA 02322. U.S.A.
www.adamsmedia.com

Paperback ISBN 10: 1-4405-3167-6
Paperback ISBN 13: 978-1-4405-3167-5
Hardcover ISBN 10: 1-4405-007-X
Hardcover ISBN 13: 978-1-4405-0007-7
eISBN 10: 1-4405-0912-3
eISBN 13: 978-1-4405-0912-4

Printed in the United States of America.

10 9 8 7 6 5 4 3 2 1

Library of Congress Cataloging-in-Publication Data
is available from the publisher.

Toxic People is a trademark of Dr. Lillian Glass.

The stories in this book are based on the experiences of real clients, but names and specifics have been changed to protect identities.

Many of the designations used by manufacturers and sellers to distinguish their product are claimed as trademarks. Where those designations appear in this book and Adams Media was aware of a trademark claim, the designations have been printed with initial capital letters.

This book is available at quantity discounts for bulk purchases.
For information, please call 1-800-289-0963.

Contents

Acknowledgments

As the saying goes, "You are only as great as the shoulders you stand on." I have been blessed to have stood on the shoulders of some of the greatest men who graced my life. These are Nontoxic Men, whom I wish to acknowledge in this book.

My late brother, Manny M. Glass, a *True Gentleman,* who lived by that creed on a daily basis. He was one of the most decent and wonderful men I ever met. I was proud to call him my brother and even prouder to call him my very best friend—may he always rest in peace.

My wonderful, brilliant, charismatic, father, Anthony Glass, whose life's goal was to raise me into being "an accomplished lady" and to fully live up to my potential. He was a man of great integrity and a man of his word, who had a tremendous amount of humanity and compassion toward others.

My mentor at the University of Michigan and the father of my field, Dr. H. Harlan Bloomer. He was both an elegant gentleman and a true scholar.

Dr. Robert J. Gorlin, my genius professor and mentor at the University of Minnesota in the field of craniofacial genetics, whose contributions to the field of medicine equal the contributions he made to everyone's life he touched, including my own.

My dearest friend and colleague, Dr. Paul Cantalupo, who gave me even greater insight into the drama of life and human behavior.

I also wish to acknowledge some other great men who touched my life along the way: Dr. Robert Huizenga, Dr. Henry Kawamoto, Dr. Juarez Avelar, Dr. Bernard Geltzer, Dr. Edward A. Kantor, Dr. James Mullendore, Dr. Alan Galsky, Mr. Robert Cassidy, Mr. Stanley Steinau, Mr. Jerry Dunphy, Dr. Jaroslav Cervenka, Mr. Weldon Rogers, Dr. Harvey Sarles, and Mr. Paul Sweeney.

Next I wish to acknowledge Paula Munier at Adams Media for her enthusiasm and support for this book, Laura Daly for her brilliant editing of this book, and Martin Jacobs for getting this book sold. I also wish to thank Matthew Glazer and the rest of the staff at Adams Media for their kindness and support.

To all of my clients throughout the years, thank you for allowing me to be of service to you. To all my supporters and fans, your love does not go unnoticed or unappreciated. I love you back!

And finally to my very best friend in the entire world, whose presence lights up a room and makes everyone she meets smile—my gorgeous and precious mother, Rosalee Glass. Words cannot even begin to express the love, respect, and admiration I have for you. I am truly blessed!

Introduction

Too many women today are dating, living with, married to, working for, or working with a Toxic Man. Who is a Toxic Man? He's a man who makes a woman feel bad about herself. He makes her feel less than she is. He is not supportive and makes her life miserable.

Most women feel stuck when they are in a relationship with a Toxic Man. They are either afraid to do anything about it or don't know where to begin to change their circumstance. This book is designed to help you enrich your awareness so that you can quickly identify, effectively deal with, and completely heal from any Toxic Man who has made your life miserable.

This book is not about male bashing. Instead, it is about empowering you to never be a victim again. You no longer have to suffer in silence. You have choices.

The Origins of the Toxic Man

In 1995, I wrote a best-selling book, *Toxic People: 10 Ways of Dealing with People Who Make Your Life Miserable*, that is still very popular today. Published in almost every language throughout the world, it continues to be the bible of how to effectively identify and deal with specific types of "toxic terrors." It was the first book of its kind to let readers know they no longer had to suffer in silence or remain victims. They now had numerous options available when it came to dealing with anyone who made their life miserable.

Because of the book's popularity, along with the popularity of other venues I have used to educate others about Toxic People™, I am humbled by the fact that the term "Toxic People™" has now become a part of today's lexicon. Pop singer Britney Spears even sang about Toxic People™ in her Grammy Award–winning song, "Toxic." As a result of reading *Toxic People*, hearing my talks, watching my television appearances, and reading my blogs, people from around the globe shared their inspiring stories with me. They described how my work on Toxic People™ opened a new horizon for them. The common theme they relayed was how it dramatically changed their lives. They no longer felt chained by the burden of having to accept the toxic person in their life as part of their fate. They now had many choices available to them.

Throughout the years, after reading tens of thousands of letters and e-mails and speaking to countless clients and audience members postlecture, it became evident that the majority of questions and comments I received came from women who had intimate, romantic, and even business relationships with men whom they characterized as being "toxic" to them. Women wanted to know not only why these men behaved so badly but also what they could do to change the men's behavior. That's how this book came about—I saw the need to give *women* specific information about dealing with Toxic *Men* in their intimate and professional lives.

Who Is Affected by Toxic Men?

Toxic Men can distress women who are rich, poor, beautiful, plain, fat, thin, tall, or short. They can make miserable women from any religion, race, or culture anywhere in the world. As you will discover in Chapter 4, movie stars, singers, models, Harvard grads, financial whizzes, political wives, attorneys, physicians, teachers, and psychologists all have to deal with Toxic Men. Women who have nurturing personalities, such as mothers, homemakers, or teachers, or those who gravitate toward professions that help others or instigate change in people, such as nurses, health care workers, social workers, and psychologists, are especially likely to come into contact with Toxic Men. You can also be affected in your career or professional life—you could encounter Toxic Men in the form of bosses, coworkers, accountants, or lawyers.

How This Book Will Help You

After you finish this book, you will be able to identify any Toxic Man who enters your life. If a Toxic Man is currently in your life, you will now have myriad options available to allow you to effectively deal with him. And, finally, if you have had a Toxic Man in your life and still bear the wounds, now you will be able to heal.

~ Dr. Lillian Glass

PART I

Everything You Need to Know about Toxic Men

CHAPTER 1

Who Is a Toxic Man?

Definition of a Toxic Man

There are three conditions that define a "Toxic Man." He is any man who:

1. Elicits negative emotions from you
2. Behaves badly toward you or doesn't treat you right
3. Makes you feel poorly about yourself, thereby affecting your behavior and your self-esteem

If you can think of a man who does one or more of these things, he is a Toxic Man to you.

Besides a family member, a spouse, a boyfriend, or a lover, a Toxic Man can be any male in your personal life, social life, or professional or work life. He can even be a man who is of service to you, such as a doctor, dentist, attorney, or CPA, or anyone with whom you do business or interact. A man who is toxic to you may *not* be toxic to another woman. (We'll discuss this further in Chapter 3.)

"Negative Emotion" Questionnaire

When a man makes you feel bad, you need to know exactly which negative emotion he brings out in you. He can bring out these emotions when you are physically with him, or even when you are just thinking about him. When you identify the specific negative feelings he brings out in you, it gives you more insight into what kind of emotional damage he is inflicting on you.

3

Think of that particular Toxic Man in your life. Answer either Yes or No to the following questions:

1. Does he make me feel angry at him?
2. Does he make me feel sad when I think of him?
3. Do I feel contempt for him?
4. Does he disgust or repulse me?
5. Am I usually embarrassed around him?
6. Does he make me feel guilty?
7. Does he make me feel ashamed?
8. Does he seem to instigate feelings of jealousy in me?
9. Do I feel hopeless when I around him?
10. Do I feel fear or am I afraid of him?

The questions you answered Yes to show you which specific negative emotion or emotions you feel in relation to this Toxic Man. It's not enough to know that he just makes you feel bad; you need to know the specific emotion that shows *how* he makes you feel bad in order to better understand his behavior.

"How Does He Behave Toward You?" Questionnaire

Now that you know what specific negative emotion he elicits from you, it is equally important to find out the reasons you feel so badly. What does he do that causes those negative emotions in you to surface? Answer some more questions to pinpoint specific behavior that makes you feel negatively about him.

SADISTIC BEHAVIOR

1. Does he say mean or cruel things followed by the words "I'm only kidding"?
2. Does he laugh at you when something bad happens or you are upset?
3. Does he make sarcastic comments?
4. Does he seem to enjoy saying things to embarrass or upset you?

5. Does he make jokes at your expense?
6. Does he seem to enjoy belittling you or putting others down?

MANIPULATIVE BEHAVIOR

1. Does he turn things around verbally, making things your fault?
2. Does he withhold affection or sex if you don't do what he wants or as a form of punishment?
3. Does he have financial troubles, often asking you for money?
4. Does he insist you did or said something you never did or said, implying that there is something wrong with your memory when there isn't?
5. Does he attempt to secretly sabotage you?
6. Does he often contradict himself in the same sentence?
7. Does he instigate trouble, fights, or problems?
8. Does he "fan the fires," making things worse?
9. Does he seem to manipulate you and others with schemes or big ideas?

DISHONEST BEHAVIOR

1. Have you caught him in lies?
2. Does he often stretch the truth?
3. Does he withhold or gloss over important information?
4. Does he have questionable business practices that could impact you?
5. Has he taken money from you without your permission?
6. Does he have late nights or unaccounted-for absences indicative of a secret life?
7. Has he cheated on you more than once?

SELFISH BEHAVIOR

1. Does he rarely go out of his way for you, except when it is convenient for him?
2. Does he rarely treat you as a priority but rather as an afterthought?
3. Is he absent or full of excuses, not being there when you need him?

4. Does he constantly talk about himself, not giving your issues much attention?

5. Do his needs come first?

6. Does he refuse to change unhygienic or slovenly behaviors that turn you off?

7. Does he rarely spend money on you or buy you gifts?

NONCOMMUNICATIVE BEHAVIOR

1. Does he often give you the silent treatment when he's upset?

2. Is getting him to open up like pulling teeth?

3. Is he distant, cold, aloof, or lacking emotion so that it's difficult to know his feelings?

4. Do you have a hard time getting ahold of him or knowing his whereabouts?

5. Is he evasive about his business or what he does?

6. Does he ignore your requests for information?

CRITICAL AND JUDGMENTAL BEHAVIOR

1. Does he put down friends and/or family members?

2. Does he constantly criticize your looks, age, weight, or behavior?

3. Does he always tell you what you are doing wrong?

4. Does he cut down his ex or speak ill of women in his life?

5. Is he critical of women in general, including their looks?

6. Does he negate or contradict much of what you say?

7. Does he relish cutting people down?

8. Does he always doubt everybody?

ANGRY BEHAVIOR

1. Does he have unresolved issues with his mother or female relatives?

2. Is he cruel or mean-spirited?

3. Does he have a "chip on his shoulder," always angry at someone?

4. Does he often speak to you in hostile, aggressive tones?

5. Does he often speak in tones sounding like he is annoyed by you?

6. Does he often talk down to you?

7. Does he yell or curse at you?
8. Does he yell or is he condescending to servicepeople and subordinates?
9. Does he make unfounded accusations?
10. Does his temper suddenly explode for little or no reason?
11. Has he ever pushed or shoved you?
12. Does he insist on getting his way and is he hostile to you if he doesn't get it?
13. Has he ever hit you or been physically abusive?
14. Does he ever shove his fist through the wall or break things when upset?
15. Does he keep everything in, suddenly exploding in a torrent of anger at you?
16. Does he give you physical jabs or slaps, saying they are "love taps"?

EMBARRASSING OR SHAMING BEHAVIOR

1. Does he cut you down or tell you what you're doing wrong in front of others?
2. Does he shout or yell at you in public?
3. Does he share your personal issues with friends, family, or strangers?
4. Is he so loud, boisterous, or obnoxious he often embarrasses you?
5. Does he talk down to you or talk at you in front of others?
6. Does he try to intimidate with his knowledge, position, or money?
7. Does he dismiss or minimize your feelings, ideas, or requests?
8. Is he overly charming to others, while taking you for granted?
9. Does he speak to strangers more politely than he speaks to you?
10. Does he call you dumb or stupid?
11. Does he shift back and forth from being nice to being mean?
12. Does he have uncontrollable temper outbursts?
13. Are you embarrassed by his drinking or drugging behavior?

CONTROLLING BEHAVIOR

1. Does he try to keep you away from friends or family members?
2. Does he always seem to tell you what to do or say, or how to dress or act?
3. Does he demand sex from you when you aren't into it?

4. Does he make you do things you don't feel comfortable doing?
5. Does everything always have to be his way?
6. Does he lecture or talk at you, paying little attention to your response?
7. Does he not let you get a word in edgewise, interrupting or talking over you?
8. Does he get involved in your business when he's not welcome to do so?
9. Does he try to convert you to his fanatical way of thinking?
10. Is he stingy with money or affection?

JEALOUS BEHAVIOR

1. Is he competitive, trying to top you with one-upmanship?
2. Does he purposely flaunt other women at you?
3. Is he intimidated by your profession, or does he belittle your job?
4. Is he wrong in his accusations about you?

If you have answered Yes to *any* of these questions, you are dealing with a Toxic Man.

"How He Makes You Feel about Yourself" Questionnaire

The final determination of whether a man is toxic to you is how he makes you feel about yourself. You know a Toxic Man has really begun to negatively impact your life when he is ruining your self-esteem. Answer the following Yes or No questions with regard to how this man makes you feel about you.

FEELING EMOTIONAL CHANGES

1. Do you feel joyless or unexcited about life when you are around him?
2. Do you cry a lot around him, especially when he hurts your feelings?
3. Do you feel hopeless, stuck in a rut, or as if life will never get better?
4. Are you frustrated by being restricted and limited?
5. Do you escape your emotional pain by eating, sleeping, or drinking?

6. Do you feel anxious or panicky?
7. Does his negativity bring you down or depress you?
8. Are you angry at yourself for letting him treat you so poorly?
9. Are you angry, irritable, annoyed, or snappy as a result of being with him?
10. Do you feel emotionally empty, especially after making love to him?
11. Do you feel that he is the cause of many of your sleepless nights?

FEELING AFRAID OR FEARFUL

1. Do you feel as if you walk on eggshells around him?
2. Are you afraid to say what you really think or feel around him?
3. Are you afraid you'll say something stupid and he'll let you know it?
4. Are you timid and shy around him?
5. Do you feel inhibited around him, including sexually?
6. Do you hesitate to tell him the truth for fear of repercussions?
7. Are you physically afraid or terrified knowing what he may do to you?
8. Do you fear his anger when you don't do exactly what he says?
9. Are you afraid he will withhold love or affection if you don't do what he wants?
10. Are you afraid he will get mad if you stay out late or if he doesn't know your whereabouts?
11. Do you fear not knowing when he is going to blow up at you?
12. Does he make the hair on the back of your neck stand up?

FEELINGS OF SELF-DOUBT

1. Are you starting to believe his negative comments and putdowns?
2. Do you now question your intelligence, appearance, and sex appeal?
3. Do you feel dumb for being manipulated or conned?
4. Do you feel that no other man would ever want you?
5. Do you always feel unsure or in doubt when it comes to making a decision?
6. Does he make you feel worthless?

FEELINGS OF PHYSICAL CHANGES

1. Do you find that you are not as mentally alert as you were before you met him?
2. Does he literally make you sick to your stomach (e.g., cramps, nausea)?
3. Does he give you a headache, backache, neckache, or other body pains?
4. Have you gained or lost weight because of him?

FEELINGS OF GUILT AND SHAME

1. Do you detest him and feel guilty for this feeling?
2. Are you ashamed and embarrassed that you are with him?
3. Do you feel guilty for explaining away his drinking or drugging?
4. Do you feel guilty if you earn more than he does?
5. Do you ever minimize your accomplishments so he won't feel jealous of your achievements?
6. Do you find yourself apologizing to others (friends, waitstaff, employees) for his behavior?
7. Are you ashamed to tell anyone how he really treats you behind closed doors?
8. Does he make you feel guilty about not doing what he wants?

NOT FEELING LIKE YOUR OLD SELF

1. Do you find yourself clamming up, with little or nothing to say?
2. Are you more wary of others?
3. Are you shaky, tentative, or fearful doing new things?
4. Do you feel he sucks the energy out of you so you can't function like you used to?
5. Do you feel insecure and tentative about yourself?
6. Do you minimize yourself so as not to intimidate him?
7. Do you feel isolated and not as social as you were before you met him?
8. Do you feel a sense of relief when you are away from him?

If a man makes you feel so badly about yourself that you experience these types of emotional changes, fears, doubts, physical changes, guilt, or shame, or if you have lost touch with your old self and who you are, you have been exposed to a Toxic Man.

Eleven Toxic Types of Men

Based on the characteristics listed in these three questionnaires, I have come up with a list of Eleven Toxic Types of Men. These Toxic Types are:

1. The Jealous Competitor
2. The Sneaky Passive-Aggressive Silent-but-Deadly Erupting Volcano
3. The Arrogant Self-Righteous Know-It-All
4. The Seductive Manipulative Cheating Liar
5. The Angry Bullying Control Freak
6. The Instigating Backstabbing Meddler
7. The Self-Destructive Gloom-and-Doom Victim
8. The Wishy-Washy Spineless Wimp
9. The Selfish Me-Myself-and-I Narcissist
10. The Emotional Refrigerator
11. The Socio-Psychopath

As you can see by the names ascribed to each of these types of Toxic Men, their dominant behavior is what defines them. That's why it's important to know what negative emotions the Toxic Man elicits in you—it's one way to figure out which Toxic Type he is. You may even recognize many of these Toxic Types from famous people in the news media, or you may recognize them from your own life or from the lives of your friends and family members.

In the next chapter, I give a detailed description of these Toxic Types, along with how to easily recognize them through their body language, facial language, voice, and speaking patterns.

Toxic Men with Mental and Personality Disorders

Some Toxic Men you encounter may also have some type of mental or personality disorder. The eleven types I describe in this book are in no way an attempt to diagnose anyone who may have a specific personality disorder. Men who exhibit several toxic behaviors may be suffering from certain disorders mentioned in the *Diagnostic and Statistical Manual of Mental Disorders* (DSM), which is published by the American Psychiatric Association and provides diagnostic criteria for mental disorders. Among these disorders are bipolar disorder, schizophrenia, schizotypical disorder, and borderline personality disorder, to name a few.

Some men exhibiting certain toxic behaviors may suffer from one or more of these disorders, and may or may not have been formally diagnosed by a licensed and qualified mental health professional. They may or may not be receiving treatment for their condition in the form of therapy and/or medication.

It is not my aim in this book to diagnose or provide treatment for any of these specific disorders. It is also essential to note that those with mental health challenges may not necessarily be categorized as being Toxic Men. On other hand, there are those who happen to have mental health challenges who may very well be Toxic Men.

Toxic Men in Business

Though I'll focus most of this book on Toxic Men in romantic relationships, Toxic Men are also present in professional and career settings. Their influence is no less significant if it is this type of relationship.

The most common scenario I've encountered in this category is women dealing with a toxic boss. His actions (or inactions) can make your day-to-day work environment miserable, and at worst, he can ruin your reputation or career aspirations. Because he is in control of your paycheck—your means of economic survival that literally puts bread on your table—there may be a lot more at stake when dealing with a toxic boss. While a toxic coworker or a toxic employee can be an annoying thorn in your side, their effect on your livelihood is not as great as a toxic boss.

For example, Patricia was a highly accomplished assistant professor loved by her students, but she could never advance up the academic ladder because of an extremely passive-aggressive Toxic Man—her boss and chairman of her department. He would smile to her face while professionally stabbing her in the back. He went out of his way to thwart her advancement as a full professor, going as low as stealing her academic research and claiming it as his own. There was nothing she could do about it because he was the boss. She could not report his actions to the higher-ups (for example, the dean) because she knew the consequences in academic politics if she made waves. She would suffer the same fate as a former colleague suffered years earlier: dismissal for a manufactured minor infraction. While she wanted to quit, as a single parent with three grade-school mouths to feed and no financial help from their deadbeat dad, she had no choice but to look the other way.

Carole was also undermined by a Toxic Man at work. But he was not her boss. She was the boss and the one who was supposed to be in charge. Yet she was so intimidated by her own male employee—a toxic bully—that he ended up controlling her as well as her business. He ran the business into the ground, rapidly losing profits. She never fired him because she was afraid of his physical retaliation. After witnessing his explosive temper flare-ups with others at work and witnessing him punching his hand through a wall when things did not go his way, the last thing she wanted to do was to get him upset with her. While she was afraid of what he was doing to her business, she was more afraid for her physical safety.

Julia was constantly undermined by a male colleague, James. He was so competitive toward her that he would stop at nothing to destroy her. He constantly blamed her for his mistakes. Julia never spoke up because she wanted to be above it, figuring the boss would eventually find out the truth. She decided to ignore what James was doing to her. Not sticking up for herself proved to be poor judgment on Julia's part, because James finally succeeded in getting her fired for one of his negligent errors. But now it was too late for her to speak up.

Toxic Men Not Only Make You Feel Bad, They Make You Look Bad

When you have a bad feeling about someone, your body leaks out information that something about that person isn't right. Your body doesn't lie and neither do your feelings. Look back at the negative feelings that you captured in the quiz at the beginning of this chapter. These feelings have a direct impact on your appearance. Whether you notice it or not, your body broadcasts signals of distress in the form of your body language and facial expression, thereby affecting your entire demeanor and appearance.

When someone makes you feel bad, it usually shows up on your face or on your body. Think of any man who makes you feel bad. Now get in front of a mirror and see what happens to your facial expression and even to your body. Are you more stiff and rigid? Are you hunched over? Is your face tight? Do your lips purse? Is your forehead furrowed? Do your eyes squint? The bottom line is that a Toxic Man often brings about toxic body language that doesn't make you shine in the best light.

Your body knows when these negative emotions are evident because your facial language, tone of voice, communication patterns, and body language reflect your feelings. The limbic system, located deep within the brain, controls your emotions. Your face, voice, speech pattern, and body language are the vehicles that outwardly express these emotions. Put them all together and you have a complete picture that expresses how you really feel.

Having a Toxic Man in your life can affect your physical appearance and how you come across to others. We have all seen examples of this in the pages of celebrity magazines, where female celebrities look more refreshed, glamorous, and even younger after breaking up with Toxic Men who gave them a hard time. We especially see it with our friends, family, and people we know.

When Martha told her friend Jackie that she broke up with boyfriend Gary, Jackie said she wasn't surprised. She noticed Martha always looked unhappy, nervous, and uptight whenever she was around Gary. Jackie now observed that Martha's brow was no longer furrowed. Jackie could now actually see Martha's eyes, which now appeared bigger. She also observed that Martha's lips were no longer tightly pursed whenever she smiled. Now she could actually see Martha's teeth when she smiled, making her look prettier. She also told Martha she observed a bounce in her step, something Martha never had when she was with Gary.

Now that you know exactly who a Toxic Man is, let's discuss what kind of women he is able to influence.

CHAPTER 2

Profiling the Eleven Major Types of Toxic Men

How I Arrived at Eleven Toxic Types of Men

As a communication expert, I have spent literally thousands of hours listening to what makes my female clients unhappy. I discovered that the number-one reason for their unhappiness was a Toxic Man who made their lives miserable. I wanted to find out what kind of characteristics made men toxic, so I conducted a study where I asked more than 1,000 women between the ages of eighteen and eighty-six to write down a list of adjectives describing Toxic Men.

The following descriptions cropped up with the most frequency: controlling, angry, meddling, selfish, backstabbing, sneaky, jealous, lying, cheating, loser, arrogant, self-righteous, competitive, wimpy, self-absorbed, self-destructive, crazy, sociopathic, manipulative, cold, mean, snobby, gossipy, psychopathic, spineless, gamer, disrespectful, and know-it-all.

Then I modified and combined several of the traits they described and created a list of eleven types of toxic terrors:

1. The Jealous Competitor
2. The Sneaky Passive-Aggressive Silent-but-Deadly Erupting Volcano
3. The Arrogant Self-Righteous Know-It-All
4. The Seductive Manipulative Cheating Liar
5. The Angry Bullying Control Freak

6. The Instigating Backstabbing Meddler
7. The Self-Destructive Gloom-and-Doom Victim
8. The Wishy-Washy Spineless Wimp
9. The Selfish Me-Myself-and-I Narcissist
10. The Emotional Refrigerator
11. The Socio-Psychopath

As a body language expert, I then created a profile for each of them, wherein I describe their body language, voice, speech patterns, and facial language so that they can be easily recognized.

1. The Jealous Competitor

Jealous Competitors try to "top" women by arguing with practically everything they say in an attempt to gain the upper hand and show dominance.

SPEECH PATTERNS

The Jealous Competitor is a man who competes with you, usually by interrupting and contradicting you, constantly disagreeing with you, or trying to "top" your stories or accomplishments. In essence, he is verbally abusive. Not only does the Jealous Competitor take the opposite point of view, he finds something critical or hostile to add, such as "You don't know what you're talking about." He may also interject additional information, just to assure his one-upmanship.

These Jealous Competitors try to "top" their mate by taking issue with practically everything she says, no matter how benign or insignificant it may seem. A simple compliment from a woman, such as, "I like that blue tie," may turn into a contentious exchange. Instead of saying "Thank you," he may respond, "The tie isn't blue. It's green. What's wrong with you? Have you had your eyes checked lately?" It is an attempt to intimidate you and put you down so that he can have the upper hand over you. It is not uncommon for him to perceive personal attacks as verbal ammunition in order to begin a confrontation with you or to intimidate you. He may do this to get a rise out of you. If you don't say anything, or say "Oh, maybe it is green" or agree with him, then he wins and you have lost in his eyes. He now perceives that he has more control and more power over you. If you argue back and say, "My eyes are just fine; you're wrong. There must be something wrong with *your* eyes. It's blue!" then he has won as well. He has you just where he wants you—fighting with him so that now he can come up with an even deeper verbal cut or more hostile comment as the confrontation has now escalated to a new and more intense level. If this back-and-forth interaction continues between the two of you, it can get very ugly and downright hateful.

Few things make you more uncomfortable than listening to a contentious Competitor Man speak to a woman. For example, Jessica told me about how she mentioned to her Toxic Man, Wayne, that she was sore from the ten-mile run she had taken. Immediately Wayne interjected, "It was seven miles," to which Jessica responded, "No, it was ten miles." "No, it was seven miles," he insisted. "It is seven miles from our house to the drugstore. I know how far it is. I measured in on my odometer." Visibly upset, she counters. "Look, I should know how far I ran. I ran it, not you." If you were listening to this conversation, you'd feel awkward. You'd pretend not to listen to this hostile exchange as you pulled the menu up to cover your face and carefully read each word as you hoped this uncomfortable exchange instigated by the Jealous Competitor would stop.

Here's another example. Mary, on a first blind date with Stephan, was bombarded with hostile questions and comments after he found out she had a PhD in art history. (He had achieved a bachelor's degree.)

"Art history!" he sarcastically remarked. "That was probably one of the easier majors. I remember I took an art course once when I was an undergraduate. It was pretty easy." Then he launched into "Where did you get your PhD?" followed by "What were your test scores to get into this grad school?" followed by "I'll bet there aren't many jobs for art historians out there" followed by "How can anyone make a living with a PhD in art history?"

All of this interrogation clearly showed that he was insecure with her having more education. It intimidated him. Therefore, he had to minimize her achievements so he would feel better about himself. Luckily for Mary, their date didn't last too long. She quickly excused herself, telling Stephan she wasn't feeling well. The final statement he made was "A lot of people with PhDs think they are smarter than everyone, but they are really not. Most of the time, they don't have much common sense." That said it all! It's a perfect example of the type of thing a Jealous Competitor would say.

VOICE

Rapid speech is characteristic of Jealous Competitors. He rarely allows you to get a word in edgewise. You will hear a lot of vocal tension as he tries to interject what he wants to say. You may also hear twinges of sarcasm, disgust, and anger in his tones as he speaks.

BODY LANGUAGE

His torso may be lunged forward in an aggressive stance, as he is literally waiting to see your next move. His rigid body posture indicates tension and conflict. He may invade your space as a means of intimidating you or pushing your buttons. When he's touching you, it isn't usually gentle, soft, and loving. Instead, it is hard, strong, and firm. He often tends to touch or grab hold of your upper arm when speaking as a way of asserting dominance over you.

Subconsciously, this says, "I want to be the dominant one." The nontender touches may also say, "I *really* don't like you and I actually want to hurt you." When a man is that dominant over you, to the extent that he uses nontender touches, it can often escalate to him physically hurting you.

To illustrate this point, I once witnessed a Jealous Competitor saying goodbye to a woman at a restaurant, giving her a short, hard, quick kiss on the lips. She wanted a longer kiss and tried to take charge and kiss him longer, but he resisted and pulled away. She wouldn't take his "no" for an answer and grabbed him and kissed him passionately. Although he finally succumbed to her kiss, all the while his hands were clenched. This is not a good sign—a clenched hand signifies hidden anger. No doubt, there is a lot of hidden anger in the Jealous Competitor, who may try at first to hide his true competitive and envious feelings. While a competitive relationship may make for a lot of passion in the early stages as the couple vies for power, control, and dominance, it wears thin over the long haul, especially when having sex becomes a competition. His underlying agitated tension, often seen through his fidgeting and physical uneasiness, inevitably surfaces.

FACIAL EXPRESSION

Because he genuinely feels uncomfortable and tense, it's not uncommon to see his eyes dart around the room. Perhaps, subconsciously, he is looking for some added advantage. As a result, it is difficult for him to maintain eye contact, which is essential for having true intimacy. Gulping or lip-licking is frequently seen when he perceives he may have lost his winning edge, no matter how insignificant. If you've clearly outshone him, "won" a new job or a raise, or even "won" in the sense that you proved you were right about something, you can expect to see a serious facial expression, devoid of emotion. He may say, "I am happy for you" or "That's great," but the truth is that he is not happy, nor is he feeling great about your win.

2. The Sneaky Passive-Aggressive Silent-but-Deadly Erupting Volcano

This man keeps it all in—he never tells you how he is really feeling. If he is upset or angry, you will never know it, but he keeps a mental scorecard. When the card is full, and he has had enough, he will explode in a torrent of anger. It may be over something insignificant, like leaving an open soda can on the counter. But his anger is not about the open can at all. It is about everything you have ever done that annoyed him since he first met you.

SPEECH PATTERNS

Like the Jealous Competitor, the Sneaky Passive-Aggressive Silent-but-Deadly Erupting Volcano may use nice words to speak to you and tell you how happy he is for you when things go your way. But the truth is, he isn't happy for you at all. He confuses you because he makes you think he's on your side and completely supports you. But out of the blue, he turns on you with unexpected criticism and sarcasm. Sarcasm is always present with this type of toxic terror. When you're least expecting it, he'll throw something back at you that you shared with him in confidence, followed by "I was only kidding" as a way of knocking you off balance and diffusing your anger. It is his passive-aggressive way of gaining the upper hand in the relationship. He doesn't come right out and say he is angry; instead, he says something mean or hurtful and tries to cover up his mean statement by saying that he was "only kidding." The truth is that he was not "only kidding." He was dead serious. Or he may make fun of something serious you once shared with him. One moment he may fawn over you as if you were royalty, and the next moment, unexpectedly take a verbal swipe at you. One moment you can do no wrong, and the next moment you are an idiot to him. Understandably, you end up not trusting him completely. How can you feel sure-footed when you don't know if you are around a friend or a foe?

There are other Sneaky Passive-Aggressors: men of few words who hold in whatever upsets them. This one never tells you what's bothering him. Instead, he'll keep a mental scorecard. He'll remember every single infraction you committed over the past five years. Then one day, when his mental scorecard is full, he will unleash a frightening torrent of vitriol. He appears to be going off on you for something as insignificant as making a rolling stop at a stop sign. But he's stored up anger against you for years, and that's really what's being unleashed. You become well aware of it as you hear the chronology of your misbehavior.

A Sneaky Passive-Aggressor rarely gives you a straight and honest direct answer when you confront him about his emotions. He may become silent or sulk. If you sense something is bothering him and ask what's wrong, he'll never divulge anything. Instead, he'll say "Nothing," "I'm fine," or "No problem." But in reality, there *is* a real problem. He's angry, but isn't going to let you know about it—at least yet. He may begin opening up and communicating, only to interrupt himself and say "Forget it . . ." midsentence. This is one of the main relationship-sabotaging tactics this Toxic Type often uses.

I knew a woman whose husband was the classic case. Stephanie was a newscaster. Her husband, Doug, couldn't be more encouraging; he sang her praises each day. He told her how great she looked, how wonderful she sounded, how bright she was. She came to rely on the daily verbal pick-me-up from her supposed number-one fan—her husband.

But then, he would forget to watch her show. When he managed to watch her show, he would sometimes make hurtful comments about how she looked like a "skinny plucked chicken" and suggested she put on weight and grow her hair. Other times he caught the show, he would tell her how gorgeous she looked and how he loved that she was so thin and sexy. One day, he would compliment her on the outfit she wore and weeks later, while she was wearing the same outfit, he would tell her how drab she looked. Of course, he would follow most of his hostile comments by saying "I was only kidding." She came to dread anything he said about her broadcasts. She never knew whether she would get a verbal kiss or a kick.

Two reasons Doug acted that way were that (a) he was jealous of his wife's success and public attention and (b) he wanted control over her because her fame made him feel insecure. So he made sure she didn't get "too big for her britches" by tearing her down from time to time. He didn't have the guts or the backbone to tell her his true feelings—that he was a little threatened by her success and notoriety and hoped she didn't leave him for someone else who was perhaps more handsome and wealthy. Instead, he gave her his passive-aggressive messages by cutting her down and building her right back up.

VOICE

Since he withholds true emotions and never gives you a straight answer, he tends not to reveal much about himself. His aim is to keep things on an even keel, not make waves, and avoid conflict, so he often comes across as benign, easygoing, and on the quieter side. This false façade often makes him a magnet for women who may also have toxic personality types such as the Angry Bullying Control Freak, Arrogant Self-Righteous Know-It-All, and Selfish Me-Myself-and-I Narcissist. If the Sneaky Passive-Aggressor is paired with any of these personality types, the results will be a lethal combination, as we will learn later on in this book.

When a Sneaky Passive-Aggressor speaks, the volume of his voice trails or dies off at the end of sentences, making it difficult to hear everything he's said. That, along with softer, quieter tones makes you always ask him to speak up. This is exactly what he wants from you. It's part of his control mechanism to get you to pay attention and make him feel important. Sometimes, it's easier to not ask him to repeat and to ignore what he said. In doing so, however, you may miss important messages and feelings he's trying to convey. A higher, overly bouncy sound or sickeningly sweet tone usually means he's overcompensating for some negative feelings he has toward you.

Another way a Sneaky Passive-Aggressor hides anger and jealousy is by not opening up his jaws wide enough when speaking, making him sound nasal and lock-jawed. He may hide anger and not give you a true read of his emotions by using a monotonous voice. Finally, a Sneaky Passive-Aggressor may laugh or cough as a sign of discomfort if he has to reveal any true emotions.

BODY LANGUAGE

In his attempt to overcompensate for negative feelings toward you, he may commit nonverbal fawning by touching you a lot. In addition, you may see him rock back and forth, which is his subconscious attempt to get away from you. Other indications that he really doesn't want to be in your presence are tapping his feet, drumming his fingers, and making other hand and foot movements that indicate he's anxious to leave. Besides foot movements, his toes may be pointed in the opposite direction when he's speaking to you. It says, "I want to get out of here."

You may also notice his hands curled up in fists, with the thumbs hidden inside the palms. This shows hostile feelings. And just as he's not revealing his true emotions through his voice and speech patterns, he's not revealing his feelings through his legs. He'll cross and lock his ankles to hold back emotions. He may also subtly jerk his head back when speaking or rub his neck, which both reveal that he's repressing his feelings.

To indicate ambivalent feelings toward you, he may quickly lean in toward you—a signal that he's interested in what you have to say—and then immediately lean back to indicate he's *not* interested in what you have to say and he's keeping his distance from you. Because he harbors ambivalent feelings toward you, he'll usually not hug you face-to-face. Instead, he'll twist his body at an angle so he's hugging you from the side. It's a way of physically cutting you off and maintaining a distance.

FACIAL EXPRESSION

A tight-lipped grin is evident in a Sneaky Passive-Aggressor, in which his lips are not turned up at the corners as usually seen in a genuine or sincere smile. You may see an uneven smile or a smirk that indicates his ambivalence. He may also cup his hand over his mouth when speaking to you, which indicates he doesn't want to tell all or reveal how he really feels. In doing this, he's holding back, just like he does when he bites on his lower lip. This behavior reflects the Sneaky Passive-Aggressor's subconscious attempt to control angry or jealous feelings toward you. These feelings are why he finds it difficult to look at you for any length of time, and breaks eye contact or gaze when talking to you.

3. The Arrogant Self-Righteous Know-It-All

The Arrogant Self-Righteous Know-It-All thinks he has all the answers. He feels that he is smarter than everyone else, that his views are the only correct ones to have, and that his moral compass is the one by which everyone should live.

SPEECH PATTERNS

An Arrogant Self-Righteous Know-It-All verbally degrades you and patronizes you in order to make himself feel that he is better than you. His putdowns are often subtle. For example, your opinion may be met with comments such as "Are you sure about that?" or "Surely you don't believe that." He may even be more direct and say such things as "You don't know what you are talking about" or "Where's the evidence to prove what you said?" There's a mechanical, rigid preciseness in his speech pattern as he tries to control conversation. He's a close-minded intellectual bully. Only his ideas and opinions matter, and no one can change his opinions or open his mind to new ideas or points of view. He's quick-tongued and seems to have an answer for everything if you try to change his mind. He usually gossips and criticizes others regularly. He thrives on making himself right and you wrong.

He often speaks in a slow, condescending manner, showing off knowledge. He talks *at* you, not *with* you. He speaks deliberately and articulates and enunciates carefully. He'll often use trendy expressions, pretentious vocabulary, or ethnic words peppered throughout his speech as a means of showing off, letting you know how intelligent he is, and how much he knows. Because he's so insecure, his biggest fear is not having an audience to whom he can be condescending. Because he's so self-righteous and thinks he knows everything, like the Selfish Me-Myself-and-I Narcissist, he uses the term "I" a lot.

He's usually so self-absorbed, he has little regard for others' time or attention spans when pontificating to them. He takes forever telling a story or expressing an idea, often ignoring you if you try to interject your opinion or ask a question. He'll often speak over you as though you weren't even there. Because it is so easy for him to depersonalize and objectify you when speaking, he is able to speak to you in a degrading manner. He often does this by verbally assaulting you with words, spoken so violently in such a staccato, disgust-laden tone you may feel as if there are verbal bullets piercing you. He thinks nothing of laughing at you, teasing, making cutting remarks and snide comments, or using sarcasm toward you if he assumes you don't understand what he's saying or you disagree. If you do manage to get a word in edgewise and complain about his condescending treatment of you, he'll belittle you and sadistically assure you that you're being too sensitive.

VOICE

The Arrogant Self-Righteous Know-It-All uses a staccato, deliberate choppy tone, devoid of much vocal animation. This gives him the tonal quality of someone who is highly critical. His hard, glottal, attacking tones reflect impatience with those whom he sees as a being subordinate. He often sounds as if he's speaking to a naughty schoolchild. If he feels that his attacking tones aren't getting through to you, he may instead speak in quieter, calm tones that force you to listen and pay attention to what he has to say. Therefore, he may be quiet and subtle or he may attack, depending on what he finds will work in terms of being able to push your buttons.

BODY LANGUAGE

If you confront him, or respond to his droning, condescending pontification, you'll often see his body language become impatient—he'll fidget and move around a lot. Otherwise, you'll see a stiff, erect, and rigid body language. He usually leans backward an attempt to maintain an air of social distance between himself and others.

He's frequently seen with his arms akimbo, placed on his hips with elbows extended. This is a body language signal for others to keep their distance. The back of his hand is usually exposed when he speaks, which indicates he may be closed off to others and that reciprocal communication and interaction isn't welcome. He may also use a pincer grip (with his thumb touching his index finger) when he speaks to emphasize his expression of preciseness in what he tries to say. When bored or annoyed with you, it is not unusual to see him twiddling his thumbs. You often see him "steeple" (when he touches his fingertips together, making a steeple), then raise his fingers in front of his chest while conveying his opinions in his know-it-all" voice. This is often accompanied by a backward tilt of the head.

He also tends to point at you when speaking to you, once again displaying a sense of superiority over you. If you get too close to him and invade his space, or if he wants to emphasize a point to you, don't be surprised if he abusively points a finger in front of you, or actually taps your chest with it.

FACIAL EXPRESSION

It's not uncommon to see the Arrogant Self-Righteous Know-It-All with a condescending smirk or a phony, forced, tight-lipped grin. These sarcastic smiles indicate that he's disrespectfully looking down at you. You'll see him literally lift his chin and look down his nose when speaking to you. He may even close his eyelids partway, raise his eyebrows, and purse his lips in an attempt to cut you off and down. Thus, eye contact and face contact is poor, as he appears to look through you. Not looking directly at you allows him to further objectify you and continue his condescending and abusive way of communicating.

If you do confront him, don't be surprised if you see him roll his eyes, indicating disgust and annoyance that you would dare question or talk back to him. This is often accompanied by him jerking his head backward, indicating that "he's taken aback." It's not uncommon to see his eyes dart around the room, seeking out people more interesting and important than you. In a restaurant, he may speak to people at nearby tables while ignoring you.

4. The Seductive Manipulative Cheating Liar

A perfect example of the body language, vocal tones, and overall attitude of a Seductive Manipulative Cheating Liar was Senator John Edwards's dance around his ABC *Nightline* interview. When asked critical questions about whether he cheated on his cancer-stricken wife or fathered an illegitimate child, his inconsistent statements, hemming and hawing, side-stepping of questions, excessive blinking, lip-licking, and nose-touching were all signals of deception.

In the interview, he had the nerve to justify his affair by lamely admitting he only had the affair when his wife, Elizabeth, was in remission from her cancer. This Seductive Manipulative Cheating Liar fooled a lot of people for a long time until the truth was finally revealed.

This type of man is overly complimentary. Even if you initially don't believe what he says, he's so convincing, you eventually start believing him. He constantly feeds your ego, so you want to be around him. He's often overly friendly and engaging when first meeting you, behavior typical of con men. His feel-good banter can change to nasty on a moment's notice if he doesn't get exactly what he wants from you. If you confront him about flirting or cheating, don't be surprised when he flips the accusation back at you, trying to make you think that *you're* the one with the problem or that you must have been imagining what you saw. With his unique ability to twist your words, he knows exactly what to say to turn the conversation to his favor.

Here's an example of how a Seductive Manipulative Cheating Liar can turn the tables on you. Julie saw Jim flirt with Wendy when returning from the bathroom. She even witnessed Jim write down Wendy's phone number, place it in his pocket, and kiss her on the lips. Furious, Julie confronted Jim. Shrugging his shoulders, maintaining a tight smile while looking straight into her eyes, he told Julie that Wendy was his soccer teammate Carlos's girlfriend and she gave him Carlos's number because Carlos was in the hospital having pins put into his broken leg. He even pulled out the napkin with Wendy's number and said, "See, she gave me Carlos's number. I don't have anything to hide from you."

He continued to weave a whole story about Carlos and how they met and how Carlos always had a weak ankle and how this wasn't the first time he was hospitalized and how Jim had to give Carlos a ride home the last time he was in the hospital. Then, Jim immediately pulled Julie close to his body and, clearing his throat, purred, "Don't be jealous, baby. You know you're my only lady," holding her in his arms, but suddenly breaking his hold for just a moment to scratch his nose.

She thought nothing of his nose-scratching or his story. She enjoyed the erotic chills that went up and down her spine after hearing his words and listening to his low and seductive tones. She desperately wanted to believe him, so she did. Jim was elated. He felt the triumph so many Seductive Manipulative Cheating Liars feel in getting close to the edge and talking their way out of their lies.

Unfortunately, this little game is played at your expense. For the Seductive Manipulative Cheating Liar, knowing exactly what to say is his way of abusively enforcing his power to feed his undeveloped, fragile ego. He feels no remorse when lying to you. He continues to lie and twist things around to make it your fault, even if literally caught with his pants down.

A Seductive Manipulative Cheating Liar always goes on the offensive. He may accuse you of cheating first when you are clearly not cheating. When he is pointing the finger at your cheating, chances are there are three fingers pointing back at him—the real cheater.

SPEECH PATTERNS

If you listen carefully to his speech pattern, you can pick up many signals of deception:

- He may repeat words and phases, such as "I went to, I went to."
- He may use longer-than-usual pauses, as he uses that time to manufacture an answer or to make up a story.
- You might hear him repeat your exact words when you ask him a question such as, "Where were you last night after you left the party?" If he says, "Where I was last night after I left the party was . . .", rest assured he has taken the time to manufacture a lie.
- If he answers your question with a question, for example, "Why would you ask me where I was last night after the party?" it may be another indicator that he isn't telling you the truth.
- A liar or a con man will often give you way too much information that you didn't request.
- He will also go off on a tangent that has nothing to do with what you asked about.
- You may also hear his speech peppered with "like, um" and "uh"s, indicating that he is lying.
- If he constantly interjects "you know what I mean?" it is his attempt to get your reassurance that you believe what he says.
- If his rate of his speech suddenly speeds up, it usually means that he is hurrying up to get all his lies out.

VOICE

One of the ways the Seductive Manipulative Cheating Liar is able to turn these tables on you is by the vocal tones he uses. His tones are often low, gentle, slow, sensuous, and seductive, and he knows how to create a sexy breathiness when speaking. Because he harbors a great deal of vocal tension as he distorts or omits the truth, his throat muscles tighten up. Because of this throat discomfort, you will often hear him regularly clearing his throat as he lies. The pitch of his voice will also tend to go up when he lies, which is also indicative of the muscle tension in his vocal cords.

One of the most telling vocal signals is hearing a creaky-sounding tone at the end of statements, which is also due to muscle tension in the vocal cords. The muscles close off the air flow as he speaks his lie, resulting in a creaky-sounding voice. There is also a change in breathing when a person lies. So you may see him take in a huge breath of air and suddenly exhale all of it, to release his tension and nervousness (he's worried that he may get caught in his lie). As a result, he speaks without an air stream, which makes a creaky sound.

The Seductive Manipulative Cheating Liar will also do a lot of fast talking, especially when he's about to initiate a con or a lie. As he does this, you may also notice a marked difference in his tone—when he is relaxed, his tone will be smooth, quiet, and seductive. But when he's about to try to lie or manipulate you, his tone changes to a rapid-fire method.

BODY LANGUAGE

The Seductive Manipulative Cheating Liar will usually shrug shoulders, shuffle his feet, rotate his feet inward to a pigeon-toed posture, tilt his head to the side, hide his hands as he speaks, fidget, and rock back and forth to express his uneasiness. Some liars may sit or stand perfectly still without moving, appearing rigid, or may place their hands on their lap without moving them.

The Seductive Manipulative Cheating Liar is likely to invade your personal space prematurely, getting physically close to you in order to let you know he is attracted and interested. He probably "accidentally" brushed up against you and let his touch linger to further demonstrate that he was interested. Since most Seductive Manipulative Cheating Liars feel comfortable in their own bodies, his relaxed stance may make you feel comfortable around him.

He may have sexually postured himself by rolling back his shoulders to expose more of his torso in his attempts to get more attention from women. To further draw attention to himself, a Seductive Manipulative Cheating Liar often plays with his hair, puts his fingers on his lips, rubs his hands or arms, and hugs or holds on to himself for no apparent reason. A form of self-stimulation, these actions give him a sense of comfort.

If you ask him a direct question like "Were you with Bob last night?" he'll rub, knead, or scratch any part of his body if he's lying to you. In doing so, he's comforting and giving himself physical relief. The more unnerved he feels, the more discomfort he feels and the more scratching, rubbing, or hand-fiddling you'll see. He may speak to you with palms up, appearing as if he's "begging" you to believe him, up as he tries to explain away his lie.

FACIAL EXPRESSION

Most Seductive Manipulative Cheating Liars who want to reel in their prey never lose eye contact and know how to hold their initial flirtatious gaze beyond the normal two to three seconds. The one targeting you probably tilts his head in your direction, nods with approval whenever you speak (whether he agrees with you or not), and mirrors your facial expressions.

He will also exhibit a number of other seductive facial movements, such as having a relaxed smile, showing his upper teeth, having a sexy slight lip pout combined with a fixed gaze, or possibly lightly licking his lips in a subtle, relaxed manner.

5. The Angry Bullying Control Freak

This toxic terror is all about controlling you by telling you what to do and how to do it. He does it by intimidating you with his anger. If you don't do what he wants, he will become more angry and more abusive toward you.

SPEECH PATTERNS

The Angry Bullying Control Freak is one of the most toxic of all the terrors. He's verbally belligerent. Constantly spewing forth hostile words and phrases, he's always ready for verbal warfare. Challenging him will usually evoke a tirade of screaming, shouting, yelling, and interrupting. He thinks nothing of verbally abusing you by flinging a barrage of degrading curse words. He uses controlling phrases such as "I'm going to let you . . ." or "I'll allow you if . . ." or "I'll give you my permission to . . . ." He'll also tell you what he won't allow you to do by using phrases such as "I don't want you to . . . ," "I forbid you to . . . ," and "You can't . . . ." In essence, he speaks to you as if you are a naughty child, telling you what you can and cannot do.

He makes many demands by speaking to you in judgmental terms, such as "No, that's wrong! Do it this way! Don't you ever listen?"

Some Control Freaks will allow you to do what you want as long as it conforms to their rules. For example, yours may say, "You may visit your mother, but only if you are back before it is time to make dinner." He'll be highly critical of what you look like, how you dress, where you go, what you do, what you eat, and how much money you spend (even if you are the breadwinner!).

He'll try to control all of your basic freedoms, often threatening you if you try to assert yourself, by commonly making warning statements like "You don't want to see me mad." Take these threats seriously—he means what he says. Unfortunately, verbal abuse can easily escalate to serious physical abuse, and even death.

VOICE

There is an alarmist quality to the Angry Bullying Control Freak's voice, as though there is impending danger. And there is! He possesses such inner hostility toward himself and others that it can't help but be reflected in his voice. He attempts to intimidate you through a loud, staccato, drill sergeant–like voice. He makes hard, glottal attacks when he communicates contempt. When you don't obey or he feels he's losing control, his tone gets louder, not caring who hears him. His main goal is for you to obey and not challenge him.

You'll never hear an upward inflection indicating a request. Instead, you'll only hear harsh, loud, demanding barks, as he takes sadistic pleasure in making you squirm.

BODY LANGUAGE

His body language reflects the same harshness and anger you hear in his voice and speech patterns. He has an aggressive body stance, appearing to lunge forward when sitting, standing, or walking. He may also invade your personal space as a means of intimidating you. His touch isn't gentle, but rather firm, very hard, or even hurtful.

He often uses a lot of arm movement, such as pointing his finger at you or your chest, or grabbing your arm when making a point. Because he's usually so angry at you and the world, it is not uncommon to see his hands positioned in a closed fist when he speaks, to forcefully emphasize his aggressive threats.

FACIAL EXPRESSION

A furrowed brow is usually characteristic of the Angry Bullying Control Freak's facial expression. His often tense expression is characterized by an intense narrow gaze and hard stare in conjunction with his flared nostrils. Usually his lips are pursed tightly, even when listening and not speaking. He speaks in a closed-jaw manner, indicating inner anger and hostility. Also as a sign of aggression, he tends to thrust his lower jaw forward.

If he's really angry, you'll see rapid eye blinking, audible breathing through flared nostrils, a flushed face, and eyes opened very wide, looking very large (where you see the whites of his eyes all around the iris). If you see these facial signals, get out of the way. It means he's about to do you great harm—he's ready to attack you.

6. The Instigating Backstabbing Meddler

The Instigating Backstabbing Meddler gets into your business as if it were his own and tries to manipulate you and your situation so that he benefits from it or he gets you to do things his way.

SPEECH PATTERNS

The Instigating Backstabbing Meddler is quick to give you his unsolicited opinions on how to run your (and everyone else's) life. He's not usually diplomatic but he's definitely highly opinionated, so he speaks critically, in bold and blunt terms. Common words and phrases you often hear him say are: "You should . . . ," "Why don't you . . . ," "Don't do . . ." or "Do . . . ," "You must . . . ," and "You better . . . ." He has the keen ability to twist your words and turn what you say against you by using confusion tactics. For example, you may have told him at one time that you don't like to exercise. He may then later use those words against you. After he hears you complain about how tight your pants are, he may say, "Well if you wouldn't hate exercising, maybe they'd fit you." Often accusatory, he'll insist that you said something you never said, meant something you never meant, or felt something you never felt. He'll exaggerate or misinterpret what you said. You can't defend yourself to set the record straight or explain what you meant because he'll insist you said something and tell you what you meant. There's nothing you can say or do to change his perception as he meddles in your truth.

He's also a huge gossip and plays the game of bringing and carrying information to amuse himself and to gain power over you. He attempts to gain that feeling of power over you by having exclusive secret information to which only he is privy.

He can also be charming if he desires, which adds to his credibility when trying to turn others against you or turn you against others. He'll think nothing of betraying anyone's confidences, including yours. If you did share a secret with him, he won't hesitate to use it against you if it benefits him in some way. For instance, if you once shared that you were a bed wetter as a child, chances are he'll bring it back up to you, just to rile you up or instigate insecurity. He thrives on this type of toxic behavior. His conversation mostly consists of saying negative things about others to you and vice versa. Rest assured that if he's constantly trashing others to you, he's trashing you to others.

He's also the master of the sarcastic quip and the backhanded compliment, where he'll give you a compliment that really isn't a compliment. For instance, he'll tell you that the necklace you're wearing is stunning and brings out your eyes so it takes the focus off of your double chin. He'll say negative things about people to cause panic, such as "You better call your brother-in-law right away and find out why he was with this blonde at the mall." Upset, you immediately call and give your brother-in-law the third degree only to find out he was at the mall buying your sister a birthday present and that the blonde was the saleslady who was old enough to be his grandmother. The Instigating Backstabbing Meddler knew what was going on, but wanted to create some drama and trouble.

He'll often talk about how clever he is as he gleefully describes how he put one over on someone, fooled someone by being so cunning, got the last laugh, or "showed that person a thing or two."

VOICE

The Instigating Backstabbing Meddler is usually fast-talking and speaks in an alarmist fashion, as though there is an urgency to do something, or danger is impending. That's how he gets you to do what he wants—confusing you by inciting your emotions and impelling you into action.

He'll often speak loudly, with a lot of dramatic animation to create excitement and maintain your interest. He may also use hushed and breathy tones when gossiping or giving you "privileged" information—as if the news is a secret for your ears only. These hushed tones are used as a means of control and manipulation. He uses these soft tones so that you will have to stop and carefully listen to what he has to say. If you don't hear him and ask him to repeat what he says, he now feels that he has the upper hand over you, as he is forcing you to pay close attention to everything he says.

BODY LANGUAGE

The Instigating Backstabbing Meddler often tends to invade your space, especially when giving you "privileged" information. Being physically animated—pacing around and using a lot of arm and hand motion—keeps you focused on him. The more he wants to alarm you, the more animated he becomes. You will see this when he insists you take immediate action, turns your words around, or tries to convince you that you said something you never said. When speaking, both his body and head move around a lot.

He also tends to point his finger a lot, especially when he tells you what you should and shouldn't do. It's not uncommon to see him pinch his thumb and his fingertips together as he tries to make a point. This gives you the visual impression that he's literally holding on to his words as he doles out just what he wants you to hear and know.

FACIAL EXPRESSION

His tendency to speak so negatively is often reflected in his facial expression. That's why you'll often see him with a furrowed brow and tight lips. When he's trying to incite you, you'll usually see a look of alarm on his face, with wide eyes and a wide-open mouth. Because he knows he's instigating trouble or telling you things that may not be true, you may see a lot of eye-blinking or lip-licking as well.

7. The Self-Destructive Gloom-and-Doom Victim

He sees the world and life as a "glass half empty" rather than half full. Because he is always looking at the negative and expecting the worst, negativity permeates his life. If things happen to be going well, he will do whatever he can to sabotage his circumstances. He sees himself as a help-less victim who can do nothing about his situation. He is his own worst enemy as he often abuses himself with one vice or another.

SPEECH PATTERNS

The Self-Destructive Gloom-and-Doom Victim is in a tremendous amount of emotional pain, which is the underlying reason he sounds so negative and feels so worthless. Perhaps his negativity is a result of a troubled childhood or not being able to cope with bad experiences that have occurred throughout his life. Maybe he mirrored this negativity from living with a parent who behaved the same way. No matter the reason for his gloom-and-doom approach to life, he can't seem to pick himself up and move ahead. Instead, he lives with the pain of his past and takes it into his present and his future. He feels like destroying himself—and, unfortunately, taking you with him.

Because he often keeps his true feelings and inner pain hidden deep inside, he'll lash out by blaming himself and others. When he lashes out at himself, you'll hear him make disparaging remarks about himself. He will tell you how dumb or stupid he is, how "it's just his luck," how everything bad happens to him, and how he can never catch a lucky break. He always complains, dwells on why things are bad, and constantly refers to his past, which gives him a bleaker view of his present and future.

He's the best excuse-maker for why things don't work out or why he's in his current position. He has a difficult time taking any responsibility for his actions.

For example, a Self-Destructive Gloom-and-Doom Victim will tell you that he is drinking because he doesn't like his job, the kids will be in college soon, the mortgage payment is huge, the stock market is bad, and so on. He claims that drinking is his only way of letting off steam. If you suggest that he look into other job opportunities, see about the children applying for a college loan, or sell his house and find a cheaper place to live, he will come up with other excuses. He is a "Yeah, but" man. Any positive suggestion is met with a negative "Yeah, but" reason as to why things won't work.

The Self-Destructive Gloom-and-Doom Victim sees himself as one of life's sacrificial lambs, and he always uses such terms to describe how much he's had to sacrifice and suffer. As a result of all his negativity, he doesn't feel worthy of good things and expects bad things to happen. If you try to help by saying something positive or encouraging, it will usually be met with a negative, self-abusive comment. He'll either ignore your compliment or words of encouragement or tell you why you are wrong and how you don't know what you are talking about.

As well as being quick to blame himself, he's quick to blame everyone and everything for his hopeless position—especially you. It's your fault he's taking drugs. It's your spending that drives him to drink. Whenever you hear "It's your fault that I'm . . . ," you can be 100 percent sure you're talking to a Self-Destructive Gloom-and-Doom Victim.

Because he doesn't have much self-esteem and feels that his relationship probably won't work out anyway, you'll often hear him say things that will purposely create hurt feelings or an argument. This is especially true when things are going along well in the relationship. He'll immediately say something to mess it up and alienate himself. Then he'll admit that it was his fault and tell you how he can't do anything right. However, he'll keep saying the same toxic things to incite disharmony, because he doesn't feel he deserves a happy relationship. It's his subconscious desire to destroy the relationship.

If he's self-destructing with drugs or alcohol, be prepared to hear a barrage of verbal attacks against you, in the form of cursing and unfounded hateful accusations. His unleashed attacks reveal internal self-hatred and agony.

VOICE

His voice sounds depressed and is a lower-pitched monotone, devoid of animation. In addition, the tone of his voice may sound weak from time to time, depending on how victimlike he's feeling. These vocal characteristics clearly reflect inner sadness and feelings of powerlessness.

His voice is especially soft when describing how poorly he was mistreated by others. When complaining or explaining, it's not uncommon to hear a nasal whine, especially as his pitch goes up at the end of his statements. Without even listening to his words, you can hear a whiny "Can you believe this is happening to poor me?"

Loud yelling and verbal abuse are not uncommon, especially if he's blaming you or someone else for his predicament. This is particularly evident if he's been drinking, drugging, or engaging in other self-destructive behaviors. You may also see tonal swings, where he goes from self-pitying, soft, whimpering tones to loud, shocking, hateful, thunderous tones in moments.

BODY LANGUAGE

The Self-Destructive Gloom-and-Doom Victim usually has poor posture with slouching shoulders, as though the entire weight of the world is on them. In using this posture, he minimizes himself. You often see him with folded arms as a subconscious means of self-protection. His head is usually bowed in a downward position so he has to look upward when talking to others.

If you try to comfort or challenge him by offering suggestions to get him out of his victim state, you'll often see a restless, rocking-back-and-forth motion. In addition, he often fidgets, picks or bites his nails, and wrings his fingers or hands.

It's common for Self-Destructive Gloom-and-Doom Victims to shuffle their feet or cross and uncross their legs. In order to comfort himself or to feel more secure, he may often clasp his hands together, or hold on to his arms or legs when listening or speaking.

There's another side to this Self-Destructive Gloom-and-Doom Victim. Because he feels so badly about himself, he'll not only take out those bad feelings on himself (by excessive drinking, eating, or drugging), he'll take them out on other people or things. That's why it's not uncommon to see him drive recklessly, punch out walls, or even punch *you* out.

FACIAL EXPRESSION

His eyes tend to narrow when speaking, due to muscle tension around his eyelids, brows, and forehead. His lips are tense, especially around the corners, which indicates repressed anger and chronic sadness. When he's feeling uneasy and anxious, you may see him bite his lower lip. He wears a consistent facial mask of tension and sadness. He'll usually look down and have poor eye and facial contact and often rotate his eyeballs downward to reflect shame. If he's been verbally abusive, he won't look at you because he may feel shame for his actions.

8. The Wishy-Washy Spineless Wimp

He can never make up his own mind about anything and is often swayed by popular opinion. He lives in fear and will never make waves or stick up for himself or others.

SPEECH PATTERNS

The Wishy-Washy Spineless Wimp can't confront people head-on, so he stays away from any communication he perceives as challenging or uncomfortable. Because he can't face direct communication, he runs from it, through silence, circumlocution (where he beats around the bush, not giving you a straight answer), or omission. He's a person of few words and chooses words carefully so as not to offend anyone. He's often afraid to confront or to be confronted, or to commit to any point of view. He'll couch everything he says in tentative terms like "perhaps" or "maybe" or "I'm not sure," or give you a preamble, presenting both points of view. He'll do it again at the end of his explanation, still never telling you where he stands. These men are "sheeple" (sheep + people) who follow the herd and do what everyone else is doing.

He doesn't have a mind of his own. For instance, if you ask who he'll vote for in the upcoming election, even though he may prefer one candidate over the other, he won't give you a straight answer. Since he doesn't want to offend or end up in a debate, he'll tell you good points of each candidate and not tell you who he prefers. He'll change the subject or turn the question back to you, asking who you prefer and why. If you press him for an answer you'll usually hear a loud sigh and possibly some throat-clearing before he utters, "I really don't know," "I'm not too sure," or "Boy, that's a tough one!", or any other phrases indicating unwillingness to commit an answer.

While he may have told you he went to dinner with a friend from high school, he omitted that it was a former girlfriend from high school, for whom he still has feelings, even if it has been more than twenty years. He's not lying out of malice or manipulation, however; he's lying because he doesn't want to deal with any ensuing confrontation.

Because he fears making a mistake or giving the wrong answer, you'll usually hear, "I don't know," "I'm not sure," or "I don't care; you decide." In his attempts to not make waves or offend, he becomes what he fears most: He becomes offensive.

VOICE

He often speaks softly and his voice tends to die off at the end of sentences, making it difficult to hear, which is his intent. Since he doesn't want to make a mistake or say the wrong thing, he'll usually speak very slowly, measuring each word. There may be long pauses between words and phrases as he carefully thinks about what he'll say before saying it. You can almost hear the fear in his voice. Therefore, you'll often hear a lot of tentative, hesitant tones, with a lot of repetition of words and phrases. These vocal habits reveal that he isn't being totally honest or forthright with you. In attempting to not offend you, he won't tell you the truth regarding what he's really thinking. Throat-clearing is also another giveaway that he's not being completely candid with you. You may also hear shakiness in the voice, especially if confronted or pressed to make a choice.

BODY LANGUAGE

You will see a lot of head-scratching when the Wishy-Washy Spineless Wimp is asked a question he doesn't want to answer, indicating confusion and discomfort. Usually he'll have a weak or limp touch because he's afraid to make the first move.

Another display of his insecurity and timidity is in his posture, which is often slouched, with shoulders positioned forward. He may also rock back and forth when he's feeling nervous or uncomfortable or uneasy in the situation. He'll also turn his toes inward as though pigeon-toed, to indicate resignation or submission. He may fold his arms across his chest or body, as a means of subconsciously protecting himself from emotional discomfort. Furthermore, he may hold on tightly to himself or an object to brace himself when confronted. His bowed head reflects attempts to avoid communication and signifies submission.

FACIAL EXPRESSION

When feeling intimidated, which is most of the time, the Wishy-Washy Spineless Wimp will go to great lengths to avoid eye contact or facial contact. He'll look to the right, left, up, or down—anywhere but at you when he's speaking. If confronted or forced to make a decision, he'll usually look down at his feet. There is often a look on his face that radiates either tension or fear. It's reflected in his eyebrows, which are usually drawn together while his forehead is furrowed. Lip biting and a retracted chin show his lack of confidence and uneasiness. Blushing of the face and blotches on the neck often occur, indicating anxiety.

9. The Selfish Me-Myself-and-I Narcissist

The only concern of the Selfish Me-Myself-and-I Narcissist is himself. He is the center of his universe and expects you to see him as the center of your universe as well. His only concern for you is in relation to how it affects or applies to him. If you can't do anything and everything for him, you are of no use to him.

SPEECH PATTERNS

The Selfish Me-Myself-and-I Narcissist has an insatiable need to talk about himself and hear praise. If these needs aren't met, you'll often hear him fishing for compliments. He'll make a self-aggrandizing comment and ask you to agree with him, such as, "I'm brilliant, wouldn't you agree?" Or he'll tell you what great things others have said about him, both to assure himself and to let you know others find him wonderful, beautiful, sexy, and fabulous.

The words "I," "me," "myself," and "mine" are most prevalent in his vocabulary. Whenever he uses the word "you," it is in the context of what you can do for him or how great you feel about him. If the topic of conversation is not the Narcissist, he gets bored and loses interest in the topic. It's difficult to have a conversation with him because he attributes everything back to himself.

For example, say you tell a Selfish Me-Myself-and-I Narcissist that you are in excruciating pain from a root canal. Instead of sympathizing, he immediately tells you about *his* trip to the dentist and how he never had a cavity and only sees the dentist for a cleaning once a year. He then gives you a detailed account of his cleaning and about the conversation he had with the hygienist. She liked his suede jacket, which he found on his trip to Argentina. As you can see, it is *all* about him.

The Selfish Me-Myself-and-I Narcissist doesn't really care about what you have to say or anything you have to interject. Instead, he'll keep talking and talking until he's done and is quick to change the subject if you keep interjecting. He only wants to talk about what interests him, not you.

He conversation reveals his sense of entitlement—for example, he likes to let you know how he can get into a club when others can't. He'll relish telling you how he always gets the agent at the desk to bump him up to first class, just to let you know he is special. Because of his need to be perceived as exceptional, he usually exaggerates everything.

Since he's attracted to vulnerable victims to whom he feels superior, he will sometimes encourage you to talk about your problems. However, he will only continue dealing with your problems if you offer a huge amount of enthusiastic adulation and appreciation for what the Selfish Me-Myself-and-I Narcissist did to help you.

He is especially partial to those who have been traumatized in former abusive relationships, because these women tend to feel needy and grateful when someone is there to help rescue them. If the traumatized victim starts to recover and stand on her own two feet and no longer needs his "help," the Narcissist is off to find the next victim, but not until he's verbally abused the ungrateful victim for no longer adoring, praising, or needing him. He emotionally punishes those whom he deems inferior to him for "letting him down" or for a perceived slight.

Abusive comments like "If it wasn't for me you'd be nowhere" or "You'd be on the streets or dead without me" are usually followed by telling you how awful you are and that you are a loser. He may pull out all his verbal ammunition to debase you and humiliate you about your faults. He won't let up until he has the sadistic satisfaction of seeing you in tears. If he really feels slighted, he may even resort to physical abuse.

VOICE

Because of his extreme need for attention, the Selfish Me-Myself-and-I Narcissist usually does whatever it takes to be noticed. That is why he often speaks in an obnoxious tone, talking and laughing loudly, all the while looking around to make sure people are noticing him. Since he likes to show off and needs an audience, he'll do this by engaging people, using a highly animated, often over-the-top, upbeat voice pattern, especially when in public. He loves being "on," since his aim is to impress you.

If he's not the center of attention, you'll hear monotonous, short-clipped tones to indicate boredom. He may even yawn and sigh if he is forced to listen to your verbal drivel that has nothing to do with him. If he feels slighted or if you aren't giving him enough attention, he may start loudly vocalizing or even yelling—like an infant.

BODY LANGUAGE

Because he's so enamored with himself, he gives off an air of confidence as displayed in his straight, upright body posture. His head is usually tilted upward, which keeps his eyes in the proper alignment to see who's looking at him and noticing him.

When he speaks to others about his one and only topic—himself—you can see him leaning in to them to engage them in conversation. As soon as the topic is no longer about him, you will see him back off and lean away. He tends to invade other people's space and take up a lot of room when standing or sitting.

To further make his presence known, Selfish Me-Myself-and-I Narcissist will use a lot of hand and arm movement and think nothing of touching others as a means of getting a person to focus his or her attention on him. Like the infant, if he doesn't get his way or feels slighted, he may lash out physically. Narcissists have been known to throw tantrums, objects, and fists. Thus, Narcissists often have the potential to become physically abusive.

FACIAL EXPRESSION

When his needs are met and he's getting attention, you see him with a genuine smile, with eyes crinkling and lips spread and relaxed. He seems to have a sparkle in his eye and lights up when acknowledged and appreciated. He has great eye contact and face contact with his "fans." He'll look directly at them and constantly scan their faces for looks of approval and adulation as he talks about himself. But if his adoring fans look away or lose interest, his happy smile immediately turns upside down into an unhappy, tight-lipped frown. If he's not the topic of conversation, a glazed look of boredom will come over him and he will visually disconnect. If he's in a relationship where he's not given constant attention and approval, his facial language will show anger, complete with knitted brow, furrowed forehead, and narrowed, steely gaze.

10. The Emotional Refrigerator

He is cold and unemotional, and lets very little of himself out. He is a man of few words, so you never know how he is really feeling or thinking.

SPEECH PATTERNS

An Emotional Refrigerator is verbally stingy. He tends to be a quiet man who speaks when spoken to. He's not the one to initiate conversations. Usually methodical and task-oriented, he plays things close to the vest, rarely betraying feelings or emotions. When confronted about his lack of expression, he'll often respond by saying, "That's just not me. I'm not that type of person," "I'm not an emotional person," "I don't like to talk much," or "I don't talk about my feelings."

Because he doesn't let you know how he feels, you're always left guessing as he leaves you feeling unsettled and unsure. He'll insist on showing love for you in other ways that make *him* feel comfortable. He isn't being abusive; he's just being who he is.

If you married an Emotional Refrigerator thinking you could change him, you were wrong. That's who he is and the way he will stay. He can only attempt to change if *he* wants to change, not if *you* want him to change. But if you married a man who was not an Emotional Refrigerator, but who turned into one and suddenly began giving you the sulky silent treatment, something is very wrong. If a man is noncommunicative, withholds affection, or doesn't respond to your emotions, it is mental and emotional cruelty. It is nothing less than abuse.

On the other hand, certain disorders may cause uncommunicative behavior. This is the case with those who may have a high-level functioning type of autism or Asperger's syndrome. Having such a disorder does not preclude them from engaging in a meaningful intimate relationship with a mate. You just have to have a great deal of awareness and acceptance. In addition, he must be willing to engage in continued behavioral therapy to improve his communication skills.

VOICE

An Emotional Refrigerator usually speaks in a monotone, which indicates detachment toward you as he depersonalizes you. Because he doesn't use vocal animation, it's impossible to decipher how he really feels about a situation. He's vocally repressed, evidencing the rigid and inflexible aspects of his personality. He'll usually speak in very clipped, mechanical tones, hyperarticulating words.

BODY LANGUAGE

Even though he's barren in terms of verbal expression, the Emotional Refrigerator may leak some body language cues. Usually, his body language is rigid, with soldierlike, still posture and mechanical gestures. This tends to make others feel uncomfortable and unwelcome because they feel as though the Emotional Refrigerator is judging them or doesn't like them.

He has guarded movement and doesn't touch that often. If he does touch or hug, it is usually stiff and awkward. Often, you'll see him cover his body with his arms or arms crossing over his chest.

His head may also be held very erectly, as further illustration of defensiveness, protectiveness, and rigidity. He tends to angle his body away from you when hugging or kissing you, which indicates that he's cutting you off from his affection. He may keep his hands on his lap or hold on to himself when interacting with others to feel more secure and in control.

FACIAL EXPRESSION

Emotional Refrigerators often have a blank or unchanging facial expression. His jaw is often rigid and his chin often retracted, indicating in a primitive sort of way that he's on the lookout for physical or emotional threats. He has poor eye contact, if any at all.

He often has a tight, controlled smile. If he feels threatened or uncomfortable, you'll often see tension in his facial muscles. If he does happen to kiss you, kisses are often quick, tight-lipped, and/or perfunctory.

11. The Socio-Psychopath

The most toxic and dangerous of all men is the Socio-Psychopath. I call this category Socio-Psychopath because according to the fourth edition of the *Diagnostic and Statistical Manual of Mental Disorders (DSM-IV)*, the definitions are blurred and sociopaths and psychopaths often share common antisocial traits. One of the main differences between the two is that the sociopath tends to be more disorganized (like the Columbine killers), while the psychopath is more methodical (like cannibalistic serial killer Jeffrey Dahmer), especially in his criminal pursuits.

Famed Canadian psychologist Dr. Robert Hare developed the Hare Psychopathy Checklist—Revised, which is a diagnostic tool of twenty traits assessed by a scoring system used to rate a person's psychopathic or antisocial behaviors. They include:

1. Glib and superficial charm
2. Grandiose (exaggeratedly high) estimation of self
3. Need for stimulation
4. Pathological lying
5. Cunning and manipulativeness
6. Lack of remorse or guilt
7. Shallow affect (superficial emotional responsiveness)
8. Callousness and lack of empathy
9. Parasitic lifestyle
10. Poor behavioral controls
11. Sexual promiscuity
12. Early behavior problems
13. Lack of realistic long-term goals
14. Impulsivity
15. Irresponsibility
16. Failure to accept responsibility for own actions
17. Many short-term marital relationships
18. Juvenile delinquency
19. Revocation of conditional release
20. Criminal versatility

If you observe these traits in your man, it is in your best interest to get away from him—he can be dangerous and your life can be in jeopardy. You cannot play around here or think you will try to change him. Socio-Psychopaths are very disturbed individuals who can cause enormous havoc in your life.

SPEECH PATTERNS

Men who are socio- or psychopathic prey on others using charm, deceit, violence, or other methods that allow them to get with whatever they want. Therefore, in terms of speech patterns, a Socio-Psychopath may try to cajole you by complimenting you excessively and speaking to you with beautiful words that you never heard from any man.

A Socio-Psychopath usually makes a great first impression because he'll say what you want to hear. He'll ask you lots of questions about yourself because he wants to quickly figure out what you want to hear and what your "hot buttons" are. He wants to know what makes you happy, mad, or sad, so he can play on your emotions, which he lacks.

But even as charming as he tries to be, he'll often leak out insensitivity by making unfeeling and even sadistic comments. At first, the comment may sound so strange and macabre that it gives you a chill when you hear him say it. Don't ignore your body's response. It is your limbic system warning you that something is very wrong! Because most Socio-Psychopaths have been cruel to animals as children, he won't like animals and may even make sadistic comments about your animal. Let's say he asks the age of your dog, you say ten, and he replies, "Isn't he supposed to be dead at that age?" When he sees the look of shock on your face, he will no doubt say, "I was just joking." Do not laugh or smile. He was *not* joking. Any sadistic comment about animals or children should be a huge red flag to you.

The Socio-Psychopath speaks of himself in very grandiose terms. When he speaks about others, it is usually to place blame and to tell you how awful the person is and what he or she did to him. He takes no responsibility and never uses the words "I'm sorry" or "I apologize." Mistakes are always someone else's problem.

But one word he'll use with frequency is "I," given his overly inflated opinion of himself. He lives with a sense of entitlement in a world that revolves around him. This makes him brag a lot and seem very cocky.

He may lie to you to get what he wants and has a complete disregard for the feelings or rights of others. Words mean nothing to him. A statement such as "I'll never cheat on you again" means zip coming from a Socio-Psychopath.

He's also highly receptive to perceived slights, so if you say something negative he thinks is directed at him, he'll react by saying hostile and derogatory things to you.

Since he's usually impulsive, he tends to live for the moment, with little regard for consequences. You'll often hear him talking about a lot of wild ideas. During a conversation, the subject matter is likely to change constantly, since it's difficult for him to stay focused on one thing.

Perhaps the most telling sign of a Socio-Psychopath is that he often contradicts himself within one sentence. For instance, you may ask, "Do you have Mr. Jones's phone number?" He may immediately answer, "No, I don't." If you pursue your question by asking, "Do you know anyone who may have his number?" he may say, "Oh, I have his cell phone number." Researchers are discovering that this contradiction in their speech patterns has a lot to do with the particular way their brain is wired.

One famous example of a Socio-Psychopath is the well-known criminal Charles Manson. Through his manipulation and "charm" (for lack of a better word), he got other people to kill for him. You can see him in action on YouTube if you search for Geraldo Rivera's interview with Manson. He used flowery, poetic prose to persuade his impressionable young followers to do his bidding. They thought he was a genius, which he verbally reinforced on a continuous basis, until they considered him a Godlike (Satanlike) figure.

VOICE

There is a deadness or a hollowness in the tone of a Socio-Psychopath. He doesn't seem to be connected. He lacks empathy, and that's why you don't hear emotion in his voice.

But you may hear a whine in his tone from time to time when he's blaming others. Since he thinks problems are everyone else's fault but his, you can hear this message in his tone of voice. If you disagree with him or have another point of view, you'll also hear the whine in his voice.

But when he's trying to manipulate you, you'll notice a shift in his normally monotonous voice. He'll get louder and the pace of his speech will get faster as he tries to get your attention. But otherwise, his deadpan tone lacks empathy and remorse.

BODY LANGUAGE

You will often find a lack of fluidity in the body language of a Socio-Psychopath. There is a stiffness and a rigidity to his movements. You may think that he has good posture, but it comes from having a rigid stance. Since movement is dictated by what you feel, and there is a void in the Socio-Psychopath's emotions, he's not able to express the full range of emotions through his body. That is why many well-known Socio-Psychopaths have a mechanical character to their movements, or make little movement at all. In fact, you often see them holding on to themselves so they won't have to express themselves through their bodies. It is not uncommon for them to speak about something positive while they shake their head "no" or speak about something negative and nod their head "yes."

Because of his puffed-up ego, you may notice a puffed-out chest, as well as a swagger in his walk, indicating he's above it all.

When he's trying to make a point, you'll see over-the-top, wide, seemingly out-of-control, large hand and arm gestures. Sometimes you wonder why he's gesturing so inappropriately. He's trying to get your attention so he can manipulate you.

FACIAL EXPRESSION

Because he lies so often and manipulates so well, pay close attention to his gaze. If he constantly looks you in the eye without moving his eyes or his head, that is a huge warning signal that he's lying to you or trying to manipulate you.

Unlike a lot of liars who break their gaze, the Socio-Psychopath will intensively stare into your eyes when he wants something from you or wants to manipulate you. There's no doubt that Charles Manson did this as he convinced his followers to commit heinous acts. You can see his intense and compelling eye gaze as you watch interviews of him on YouTube. When he wanted to make a point with Geraldo or another interviewer, he looked right into their eyes; otherwise, he consistently looked away. When a Socio-Psychopath has nothing to gain from you, he'll have a hard time looking at you because he can't relate to you as a person. He can only relate to you as an object—what you can do for him.

What these Socio-Psychopaths do is use "intermittent operant conditioning," which is when a person intensely gazes at you, then suddenly ignores you, with no eye contact. This technique compels you to listen or at least to pay attention to him, so you wait for his burst of attention. He can read your anticipation as well. That is how he manipulates you.

Facially, he lacks animation and appropriate emotional response. Often, you may see a masklike facial expression that actually looks rather pleasant because he has trained himself to keep a pleasant expression on his face to avoid showing the unpleasantness that is lurking in his mind. Because he's devoid of emotion, it is impossible for him to show a wide range of emotion through his facial expression. That is why serial killer John Wayne Gacy, who murdered many young boys, lured them by painting his face as a happy circus clown.

If a man shows a complete lack of facial expressions, that should raise a red flag for you. Unless the man's face is Botoxed, he must show *some* facial animation. But in the case of the Socio-Psychopath, he's devoid of emotion, so that is why he has difficulty showing a range of emotion in his facial expression.

Sometimes he'll try to feign emotion by crying in order to garner sympathy. But you will rarely see tears. Since he has no feelings, which includes his having no sadness, he will often mimic crying behavior by wiping under his eyes. The giveaway that he may be a Socio-Psychopath is that there are no physical tears to wipe.

CHAPTER 3

You May Be Allergic to Certain Types of Men

Each Woman Has Her Own Allergies

While you may think a man with specific traits is toxic, and have a very bad reaction to him, other women may not find that same man toxic to them, based on their personality makeup and what they can or cannot tolerate. For instance, you may find those who are silent (men of few words, men who avoid conflict at any cost) to be extremely toxic to you, while someone else may not find these traits to be toxic at all.

You may be amazed by how your girlfriend can tolerate her braggadocio husband who always talks about himself. There is no way you could ever be in the same room with him longer than ten minutes, let alone be married to him for a lifetime. But it doesn't bother your friend at all. When you recall any men you dated who exhibited these boastful and self-absorbed tendencies, you remember that you had a miserable time—those first dates were usually also *last* dates. There was no way you could tolerate being around them. And if you look back and determine why your last boss was so annoying to you, it was because he had those same traits. You could barely stomach it whenever he bragged about how great he was or how he was the best at everything. Based on your particular personality traits or what you specifically find repulsive, these are the men I would say you are "allergic" to. Being around them brings out the worst in you, though they may not bring out the worst in someone else.

The old saying "Someone's trash is another's treasure" applies here. What is toxic to one person may be nontoxic to another. So whom you deem to be a Toxic Man is very much based on your personal view of what particular traits bring out the worst in you.

What Are the Traits of the Toxic Men in Your Past?

A key part of learning how to deal with Toxic Men in the future is to understand the Toxic Men from your past. It is essential that you pick out specific traits or adjectives that are specifically toxic and intolerable to you. If you look back at the Toxic Men who have been in your life, you will probably find that specific types of men with specific personality traits whom you chose, or by whom you agreed to be chosen, surface time after time.

If you review your dating or even your marital history, you will see how Barry is Paul is Steve. Barry is controlling, arrogant, and disloyal. Paul has traits of being controlling, a know-it-all, and emotionally empty. Steve is a control freak, anal retentive, and a know-it-all. All three men seem to share something unpleasant in common: They are all controlling and seem to be know-it-alls. If you haven't been able to get along with Barry, or Paul, or Steve, you will probably never be able to get along with any man who shares the common traits of these three men—being controlling or being a know-it-all. In essence, you are allergic to men with these characteristics. If you get involved with them, you will definitely have a bad reaction, just as you did with Barry, Paul, and Steve.

While the men may be packaged differently, their underlying toxicity is the same because their fundamental personalities are similar. They are essentially the same type of person. You may have shared different experiences with them, but the results are always the same—turmoil and unhappiness. Based on your own personality makeup, there are men with whom you will simply never jell. If you do try to mix with them, the results will be disastrous.

Once you know the specific type of men to whom you are allergic, you can keep your eye out for them. If one shows up in your personal life, you can avoid him at all costs. If one appears in your business or professional world, rely on your knowledge and experience to guide you. You know what worked and didn't work in the past, so use that knowledge to make an educated decision. You can either choose to not do business with him, or tread cautiously with a lot of boundaries and contracts for your own safety and peace of mind.

"Men I Am Allergic To" Quiz

1. Make a list of ten men who made your life difficult throughout the years. Try to recall every boyfriend you had from grade school through high school and beyond, and every man who has made you miserable. Be sure to include those who are presently in your life. If you can't think of ten men, think harder; most of us can. Besides a boyfriend or spouse, it could be your father, brother, cousin, a teacher, a waiter, an attorney, a colleague at work, a physician, a dentist, or a neighbor.

2. Next to the names of each of these men, write down the top three adjectives that first come to mind. Don't censor anything; let your descriptions flow. If you are having trouble coming up with specific adjectives describing these men, use the list of adjectives on pages 58–63 to help you describe their characteristics.

3. Now compare the adjectives you used on each of these ten men. Which traits appear most often?

What normally happens when doing this exercise is that you will see that many of these men have the same negative characteristics. The more negative traits they share, the higher the chance that any man with those characteristics will be toxic to you.

For instance, my client Maureen listed the names of ten men in her life who made her miserable at one point or another. The adjectives that kept resurfacing with the majority of these men were "bullying," "controlling," and "lying." These characteristics started early in her childhood, with her brother, and ended with her present husband, from whom she is now seeking a divorce.

Because Maureen is now aware of which traits she is allergic to when it comes to men, she knows that whenever she chooses to begin dating again, she needs to steer clear of any man with any tendency to control or bully. This knowledge gives her an immense amount of power and control over her future.

In addition, Maureen is now aware that she is also allergic to her boss. Now she knows why she can't stand him! Because of her newfound information, she knows that it will always be a problem for her to work around men with these characteristics. However, she needs to keep her job, despite the fact that her boss is a controlling bully. So she has modified her own behavior in an attempt to avoid conflict as much as possible. She stays out of his way as much as she can and consciously tries not to react to his bullying personality. She knows that her paycheck is more important than liking her boss, so she goes out of her way to get along. You'll learn more tactics like the ones Maureen is using with her boss in Chapter 14.

LIST OF NEGATIVE DESCRIPTIONS OF A TOXIC MAN

abusive	anxious
acrid	apathetic
acrimonious	argumentative
addictive personality	arrogant
adversarial	attacking
aggressive	backstabbing
alcoholic	bad-mouthing
aloof	belittling
amoral	betrays confidences
anal retentive	bickering
angry	blaming
annoying	boring

bossy

brash

brown-nosing

bulldozing

bullshitting

chatterbox

cheating

cheap

clandestine

clinging

cold

commit phobic

competitive

complaining

condescending

confrontational

conniving

contradicting

controlling

cowardly

crass

critical

crude

cruel

defeatist

defensive

defiant

demanding

denying

depressed

desperate

difficult

dirty

dishonest

disloyal

disrespectful

distant

dogmatic

double-crossing

doubting

drug-addicted

dull

dumb

duplicitous

easily influenced

eggheaded

egomaniacal

egotistical

emotionless

empty

enigmatic

evasive

evil

exhausting

extortionist

fake

fanatical

fastidious

fault-finding

fearful

flamboyant

follower

forceful

foul-mouthed

fragile

frightened

frightening

gossipy

grabby

gross

guilt-ridden

gullible

gutless

gruff

harsh

hasty

hateful

helpless

holier than thou

hot and cold

hot-tempered

hurtful

hyper

ignorant

immature

impotent

indecisive

indifferent

indirect

indiscreet

inexpressive

insane

insecure

insensitive

intense

interfering

intimidated

intimidating

invasive

irrational

irresponsible

irritable

irritating

jealous

judgmental

know-it-all

lackadaisical

lackluster

lawless

lazy

lecherous

lethargic

lifeless

limited

loner

loser

loud

lying

macabre

macho

maniacal

manipulative

masochistic

mean-spirited

meddling

mercurial

messy

meticulous

miserly

moralizing

morose

mysterious

narcissistic

nasty

neat freak

negative

nerdy

nervous

neurotic

nitpicking

no boundaries

nonconfrontational

non–risk taking

nosy

not serious

obnoxious

obsessive

obsessive-compulsive

obstinate

old-fashioned

opinionated

ostentatious

overeating

overly confiding

overly neat

overly talkative

paranoid

passive-aggressive

perfectionist

petty

phony

pontificating

possessive

precise

pretentious

promiscuous

provocative

prudish

pushy

questioning

quiet

raunchy

rebellious

repressed

ridiculing

rigid

rough

sadistic

sarcastic

secretive

seductive

self-absorbed

self-deprecating

self-destructive

self-important

selfish

self-righteous

sexless

shady

shallow

shameless

sharp-tongued

sheepish

skeptical

slacker

slick

slimy

sloppy

slovenly

slow

smarmy

sneaky

snobby

snotty

socially inept

spineless

stick-in-the-mud

stingy

strict

stubborn

stupid

submissive

superficial

suspicious

tenacious

testy

thick-headed

threatened

timid

troublemaking

turncoat

two-faced

type-A personality

unapologetic

unappreciative

unaware of others

uncaring

unclean

uncommunicative

underestimates others

underhanded

unemotional

unevolved

unfriendly

unimaginative

unkempt

unmanly

unpredictable

unrealistic

unreasonable

unscrupulous	vulgar
unstable	weak
untrustworthy	whiny
uptight	wimpy
user	wishy-washy
vacuous	withholding
vapid	worrisome
venomous	yeller
victim mentality	yellow-bellied
violent	zealot
volatile	

You Can't Cure This "Allergy"

If you happen to be involved with a man you're allergic to, chances are he's allergic to you as well. That means whatever you try to do in order to win him over or change him is worthless. You may even both know instinctively, without any words being said, that you are not right for one another either personally, professionally, or both. So stop wasting your time trying to achieve the impossible because you can never win him over. If you're not sure but you suspect you might be allergic to someone, take a moment to go back and complete the "Men I Am Allergic To" Quiz and see if any of his traits match those of Toxic Men in your past.

Knowing this and taking it to heart is freeing. It will save you a lot of wasted energy, as it did for Diana, who had a business partner to whom she was clearly allergic. He kept holding back the growth of their business because he was wimpy, non–risk taking, and noncommittal. She did everything possible to try to get him to make a business decision that would help move the business forward. He wouldn't budge. She had the same issue in her personal life, where she was involved with a man who wouldn't commit either. They had been dating for five years. She wanted to move forward with marriage and children but he wouldn't budge. She worked as hard on getting her boyfriend to commit as she did on getting her business partner to commit, both to no avail.

As soon as Diana realized that she was getting involved with the same type of man over and over again, and that her business partner and her boyfriend were one and the same, she immediately put a stop to it. There was no more overcompensating and going out of her way to make things work with these impossible men in impossible situations. She quit both of them. As a result, she discovered she was a lot happier, had more energy, and even had more free time. So she used that energy and free time to do something she always wanted to do—skydive. While doing something she really loved, she finally met a man who was worth her time and energy—her nontoxic skydiving instructor!

PART II

Why You?

CHAPTER 4

Toxic Men Can Happen to Any Woman

Toxic Men Hurt All Kinds of Women!

Beautiful, talented, smart, rich, or famous—it doesn't matter how you look or how much you have in terms of gifts, brains, fortune, or fame. Any woman can get involved with a Toxic Man, as you will see in the examples throughout this chapter. Some women have no clue how they got involved with a Toxic Man, while others have consciously sought them out for one reason or another. This information may provide you with more insight as to how that Toxic Man got into your life in the first place.

Mothers

Women in the ultimate caregiver role are often susceptible to attacks from Toxic Men because they are caring, accepting, and nurturing and they make things work. No matter how they are feeling or how inconvenient the need is, they make sure that certain things are always done, such as cooking, cleaning, laundry, errands, and transporting kids to school, doctor, dentist, soccer practice, and ballet classes. Mothers have to handle children's tantrums, wipe their tears, clean their vomit, tend to their scrapes and cuts, soothe hurt feelings, and break up squabbles. In order to do this effectively, mothers apply patience. They learned early on that, even when things don't go just the way they want, to survive in their role as mother and homemaker they have to constantly exercise patience and flexibility.

While these positive qualities of excess patience and flexibility may be a benefit in child rearing, if they are carried over to an intimate relationship, they may not be such a good thing, especially if you find that you are always bending or caving in to the whims and desires of a Toxic Man. In doing so, those two positive qualities can become a detriment. While you may put up with a bit of cheekiness, sulking, sarcasm, and back talk from your child from time to time, you never need to put up with it from a grown man.

Teachers

Women in the teaching profession often find themselves victims of Toxic Men because they love to teach and instruct. They like to show people how to do things. For certain types of men—control freaks, bullies, or constant critics—having anyone teach or instruct them sets them off in a toxic way. They may become verbally abusive or contentious. Because the teacher is commonly used to these types of challenges from students in the classroom, she may ignore this type of toxic behavior from her man until it is too late.

Those Who Work Professionally to Help Others

Many women work in fields where their main role is to help others, such as nurses, health care workers, social workers, and psychologists. These women may feel that their expertise gives them an added advantage in that they have insight into how to deal with people who have problems or who are challenging. Because of the success they experience with clients in their professional lives, they feel invincible. They have no doubt that they can do the same thing in their personal lives. These women are greatly mistaken.

When they are in positions of authority and in positions where they can help their clients or patients, they succeed only because their clients want to be helped. Their dates, lovers, boyfriends, or husbands are *not* their clients. They did not come to them for help and have no intention of being helped or changed in any way.

Since the therapist, social worker, and counselor mindset is all about help and change, their good intentions are often met with resistance when it comes to their men. To boot, there are insecure Toxic Men who are so intimidated by their knowledge, level of education, and perceived one-upmanship that they become aggressive, hostile, and defensive.

Since nurses, therapists, social workers, and counselors are often used to dealing with these personality characteristics, they often accept them with the idea that they will eventually be able to modify their man's negative traits. When modification of the bad behavior doesn't happen, but gets worse, these women are often devastated.

Take Gwen, a registered nurse. She was used to cantankerous old men in her cardiac unit. She was used to their hostile tones and demanding ways. She was also used to her success rate of having these grumpy old men ending up adoring her after they received a steady diet of her consistent and unwavering warmth, cheeriness, humor, and kindness. So when she got involved with Frank, fifteen years her senior, she thought nothing of his gruffness and demanding control-freak ways. She knew that it was only a matter of time before her positive energy and daily doses of love, affection, and smiles could conquer his toxic ways. But weeks turned into months that turned into years and Frank's behavior got worse and worse. When his verbal abuse tuned into physical abuse, she knew she had lost the battle and that nothing she did could ever change this Toxic Man.

The Princess

Women who are like princesses are those who appear to have it all—sophistication, class, beauty, and money. Yet even if you have all those assets, you are still susceptible to falling victim to a Toxic Man. Why? Because you may think that you are entitled to the life of a princess. You may have even bought into your childhood fantasy of finding that Prince Charming whom you have been looking for all of your life to rescue you and to take care of you, even though you may not need rescuing or having someone take care of you. You want someone to treat you like a princess, and you'll keep looking until you find it.

Unfortunately, you may mistake a man's catering to your every whim as being treated like a princess, when in fact he is manipulating you to get what he wants out of you—fame, money, connections, or your lifestyle. Not looking deeper and doing diligence on your "prince" can land you in the same situation as award-winning actress Anne Hathaway, who played a princess on screen and off screen. Although her boyfriend, Raffaello Follieri, treated her like a princess, showering her with luxurious gifts and trips, he did not turn out to be her "prince" after all. In fact, he was a manipulative con artist who swindled others out of their money to support his impressive lifestyle. (He is now in jail.)

The Bright and Brilliant

Women who are highly educated may seem too smart to miss the warning signs of a Toxic Man. But no matter how many degrees hang on your wall, until you learn the ins and outs of Toxic Men, you will still be vulnerable to their attacks. You are not immune to them simply because of book smarts. Matters of the heart and mind are a lot more complicated.

One bright woman who had the rug pulled out from under her was brilliant Sandra Boss, a financial whiz and a partner in a prestigious financial firm in London. But even with all of her financial wisdom, she did not even know the true identity of her husband—the man she lived with for twelve years. It was only after she decided she had enough of her control freak husband, whom she knew as Clark Rockefeller, and filed for divorce and custody of their young daughter, that Sandra found out the truth. When "Clark" tried to kidnap their daughter, it was the FBI who informed Sandra that her husband was not Clark

Rockefeller, a Yale graduate, whom he claimed to be, but rather a German named Christian Karl Gerhartsreiter, who also used a multitude of aliases. He now sits in jail on a charge of kidnapping his daughter and assaulting a social worker.

The Talented

Even women with immense talent in a particular area (music, art, teaching, and so on) are vulnerable to an attack by a Toxic Man. No matter what your talent, a Toxic Man is not likely to appreciate it because of his ongoing attempts to make you miserable. Not only will you suffer, your performance may suffer as well!

Gorgeous pop singer Robyn Fenty, known to fans as Rihanna, falls into this category. Though she is a talented singer, her former boyfriend, singer-actor Chris Brown, pummeled her face and tried to push her out of a car. Why? Because she confronted him about another woman who continued to contact him on his mobile device. Initially, Rihanna blamed herself and stood by her man. But then this twenty-year-old finally wised up by letting her toxic abusive boyfriend go. After a court hearing, Chris Brown, who plead guilty, is not allowed within a specific number of feet of her and had to pick up trash along the highway and be on probation for five years as part of his sentence.

The Young

Men can be toxic at any age, so just because you are young does not mean that you won't know any Toxic Men. In some cases, lack of experience dealing with men can cause a young woman to be extra vulnerable, which is one of the reasons the information in this book is so important.

The Elderly

If a woman hasn't been with a man in a while, she may get desperate for love and physical affection. Because of that desperation, she may close her eyes to the reality of who is standing before her—and it could be a Toxic Man. She may ignore his true motives, especially if he is a lot younger than she is. While the "cougar" concept (the older woman with the much younger man) may be liberating to a lot of women, it is also fraught with a lot of potential problems that need to be carefully examined ahead of time. For example, in difficult economic times, many young men resort to finding a "sugar mama" to support them.

The Financially Vulnerable

Just as elderly women will put up with a lot for the sake of having a man in their bed, so will a woman who has fallen upon hard financial times. It's not uncommon for women to settle and accept toxic behavior from a man if it means food in her stomach, a roof over her head, and clothes on her back. Unfortunately, in times of economic uncertainty this happens more often. When her children's welfare is at stake, many women will bear the torture of dealing with a Toxic Man if it means allowing their children to survive.

The Political Wife

You don't have to be a senator's wife to be married to a toxic politician. There are Toxic Men in every level of local and regional politics. Though your life is lived in the public eye, you are not immune to the threats of a Toxic Man. Your husband's position may mean he travels a lot, or he may encounter women who are enthralled by his level of power. These influences may exacerbate toxic traits.

Look at Elizabeth Edwards as an example of a woman married to a toxic politician. This Toxic Man cheated on Elizabeth while she was undergoing a valiant struggle against cancer. Though she initially stuck by her husband after he admitted to infidelity and fathering a child with his mistress, she eventually decided to leave him.

The Beautiful Famous Golfer's Wife and the Academy Award–Winning Actress

Well, this category probably doesn't fit many of you readers, but it's still valuable to learn about. Elin Nordegren was the stunning blonde Swedish wife who loyally showed up at her famous golfer husband, Tiger Woods's, championship matches with her infant son and toddler daughter in tow. For years, while Elin stayed in Florida, caring for their home and for her kids, Tiger was having sex and partying with dozens of sex partners. While others had wind of Tiger's cheating ways, Elin had no clue her husband wasn't being faithful until one Thanksgiving day, when she allegedly found text messages to one of his mistresses on his phone. What happened next, only Elin and Tiger will ever know. Elin promptly removed her ring and sought out legal counsel. While Tiger was in "sex rehab," he took a brief respite to give a monotoned, monofaced, and mono–body language apology to his sponsors, his foundation, his fellow golfers, and his fans, finally mentioning Elin.

The same thing happened to actress Sandra Bullock. She sang her husband's praises in her Academy Award speech, looking lovingly at her biker reality-star husband while telling the world how she finally knew what it is like to have someone "have her back." Days later, it was revealed that he had actually *stabbed* her in the back by cheating with many women including a Nazi-tattooed stripper. After Bullock also discovered a photo of him in a Nazi hat making a Nazi salute, she left him and decided to raise their adopted baby without him.

The lesson? Beauty, power, money fame—none of it makes you immune to an encounter with a Toxic Man.

If She's So Smart and Beautiful, Why Did She Get Involved with a Toxic Man?

Each of the above case examples clearly illustrates how getting involved with a Toxic Man can happen to anyone—regardless of their race, age, religion, education level, socioeconomic bracket, intelligence, popularity, or physical appearance.

Whenever I hear comments like "If she is so smart, how come she got involved with such a jerk?" or "She's so beautiful, she could have her pick of anyone—why did she end up with that loser?" it makes me cringe.

Choosing the right man has everything to do with having the right information and knowledge and knowing exactly what signs to look for. You do not want to end up like these women because you have consciously or unconsciously ignored the warning signs. You do not want to fool yourself into thinking that you can tolerate him or change him, nor do you want to mistake the man you want him to be for what he really is until it's too late. As we progress through the book, you will learn how to accurately read warning signs so you will know what to look for.

The Tragedy of Women with No Choices

Throughout history, in many cultural traditions around the world, women had little or no say in picking the men they spent their lives with. While these traditions have become antiquated in many parts of the world, they are alive and well in others, such as India, Pakistan, and various parts of the Middle East, Africa, and Asia. Often, these women have little or no choice as to whom they will marry, who will father their children, how they will be treated, or what their eventual fate in life will be.

Some of these women are fortunate enough to be paired with a good, decent man. If, on the other hand, they are matched with a Toxic Man, their life will be a torturous hell. Unfortunately, in most of those instances, there is little, if anything, these women can do about it. Cultural mores, social restraints, and even specific laws often render them helpless. For those few who do dare to rebel and speak out, the price is often death. While change has come about in many of these cultures and societies, the reality is that change is slow and it may take generations before significant progress is made.

Lie Down with "Dawgs," You Get Sleaze

We've all heard the expression "if you lie down with dogs, you'll get fleas." Similarly, if you associate with a Toxic Man—a real "dawg"— you'll get "sleaze." Your life may be going along fine. You may have a good job, plenty of money in the bank, nice friends, a wonderful family, and everything working well for you. Then a Toxic Man infiltrates your life. Suddenly, his toxicity has devastating consequences on your world. It can turn every aspect of your life upside down.

Take Leslie, forty-three, a financially successful former beauty queen turned corporate executive. She became a mere shell of herself after Toxic Burt got his clutches on her. After only a year of being together, she lost her looks by turning her pain inward and eating enough to gain fifty pounds. She lost most of her friends and acquaintances because they were sick of hearing her complain about how horribly Burt treated her. She lost her job because she could no longer focus on work. She lost a lot of her savings, spending it on therapy bills, and most important of all, she lost her self-esteem. She lost so much of herself and her life while dealing with her Toxic Man. Sadly, the longer you are with a Toxic Man, the higher the price you pay— whether in financial ruin, physical pain, legal trouble, social isolation, or all of the above.

While there are many options available to you when it comes to dealing with a Toxic Man in your life (as you will discover later on in Chapter 15), realize that there are tragic things that can happen to you if you choose to stay with him.

YOU COULD GO TO JAIL

I was once on a panel of women who were involved in a program that gave inspirational workshops to women who were incarcerated. Famed attorney Gloria Allred and actress Jane Fonda were also on the panel with me. While giving my talk at the Women's Correctional Institute in Chino, California, I spoke to a number of women who were there as a result of doing something that was precipitated by associating with the wrong person—namely a Toxic Man.

One of the prisoners, a young fresh-faced twenty-something blonde, once had a life of dreams ahead of her. She shared with me the reason she was now behind bars. Apparently, her former boyfriend asked her to drive him and his buddies to a specific location, wait, leave the doors of the car open and immediately take off as soon as he and his buddies got back in. Doing exactly what he said to do, she thought it was just another one of the wild and crazy pranks he often did when he was around his buddies. It wasn't until a police chase ensued and she was arrested and charged that she realized what had taken place. She was devastated when she was found guilty of conspiracy for driving the getaway car during a robbery. It didn't matter that she had no idea a robbery was about to take place. She simply did what she was told by her toxic boyfriend and now has to pay the price by sitting in a prison cell for the next decade.

YOU COULD PAY THE ULTIMATE PRICE

The sad reality is that some Toxic Men make the women they prey upon pay the ultimate price—their life. These situations are unfortunately more common than you may realize, and they're a difficult lesson about what can happen if a Toxic Man loses control. The rate of fatalities resulting from domestic violence around the world is staggering. According to the Stop Violence Against Women Project, sponsored by the Advocates for Human Rights, 40 to 70 percent of women murder victims are killed by an intimate domestic partner, and statistics continue to grow. The reason for this broad range is that statistical information on the prevalence of domestic violence throughout the world is still difficult to obtain.

Millions of women around the world are victimized by Toxic Men who engage in a cycle of abuse, from verbal to emotional to physical. The information in this book will help you recognize the warning signs so that you will stop making excuses and get away from your Toxic Man as quickly as possible.

CHAPTER 5

How Does Imprinting Affect Your Decision-Making?

Imprinting and Its Effect on Making Choices

In this chapter, you will learn about the effect that imprinting has on choices you make—both good and bad. Imprinting is a rapid learning process that occurs early in life, whereby species-specific patterns of behavior are established. It is where the very young establish a behavior pattern of recognition and attraction to their own kind or to a substitute or an object identified as the parent.

Imprinting based on early childhood, prepubertal, and pubertal experiences may have a tremendous influence on the type of man you choose later in life. One reason women may form relationships over and over again with men who are poor choices for them is their early childhood experiences. Freud said, "What we don't resolve, we often repeat." This is the case when a woman consciously or unconsciously seeks a man with many of the same toxic qualities of her dad or mom. We often seek what feels familiar and what we know—good *and* bad.

Imprinting in Early Childhood

It is not uncommon to pick a mate who is like your father—or your mother, for that matter. The behavior your father or mother modeled for you when you were growing up is what you're used to, and what you became comfortable with or conditioned to. So when you begin seeking a romantic relationship, you often look (consciously or subconsciously) for someone with those same qualities. This can be a good thing, if your mother or father is trustworthy, honest, caring, and loving. But if your father or mother had some more negative qualities—for example, distant, abusive, or controlling—it may not be a good thing.

According to researchers, the most critical imprinting period occurs within the first five years of a child's life. As researchers have shown in experiments with geese in the classic Konrad Lorenz imprinting experiments, the effects are irreversible when a young animal or human has been imprinted upon during this critical period for learning. That is why if a child has been imprinted with being abused, it is extremely difficult for that child to not be drawn to those abusive cues or reminders later on in life.

According to specialists in the field of domestic abuse, this explains why so many victims typically return to their abuser even after repeated abusive incidents. In cases where the victim finally breaks away from her abusive perpetrator, it often takes from seven to twelve breakups and reunitings before the victim can teach herself to avoid the harmful cue or behavior.

Beautiful Barbara, who could have had any man in the world, chose abusive Jed as her husband because of the negative effects of imprinting. He barked commands and spoke to her in a condescending and impatient tone. He even made embarrassing and cutting remarks about her in front of their friends. She relayed to me how he would push and shove her as well. Once, he literally dragged her out of a store when she wouldn't come out when he called her name. The good news was that she kept breaking up with him. The bad news was that she kept getting back together with him.

One day, Barbara shared with me how her father was exactly like Jed. When she was a teenager talking on the phone, her father grabbed the phone out of her hand, hung it up, grabbed her by the hair, and shoved her into the car because they were late for a family outing. Unfortunately, since Barbara was imprinted with such negative conditioning in her childhood, she learned that it was okay for a man to cut her down and drag her and pull her hair and shove her. So when husband Jed did it to her, even though she didn't like it, it felt familiar to her. It was something she knew from her past experience. The familiar is what compelled her to keep returning to Jed, even though he treated her badly.

This pattern is not uncommon for women who date or marry abusive men. The parent was the role model for abuse. In a Freudian sense, the child ends up being attracted to the personality of that abusive father or mother, thus confirming Freud's truth in "What we don't resolve, we repeat" as we subconsciously want to right the wrong that was done to us when we were helpless and powerless as a child. As an adult, a person may subconsciously choose a partner that was similar to an abusive parent in order to work out the trauma he or she may have experienced as a child. Adults have a say and can respond appropriately.

Imprinting in Puberty and Its Effect on Your Future Love Life

After the first five years of childhood, the next most crucial point in a person's development in terms of imprinting occurs during puberty or in the teenage years. Just as a child's imprinting by his or her parents can influence dating and mating choices later in life, imprinting during the teenage years can influence physical and emotional choices in picking a mate as well.

The crushes you have, the dates you go on, and the subsequent experiences—both positive and negative—that you have when you first begin dating can stick with you for the rest of your life. That wisecracking boy in the front row who always made you laugh in seventh grade, or that bad boy in high school who was always kicked out of class, or that jock who gave you that first wink and nod of approval may be the reason why as an adult you are only attracted to funny men, untamed "bad boy types," or athletic men. When your hormones start developing and you start paying attention to who and what makes your heart beat a little faster, your tummy get queasy and your head gets lighter whenever you are around a certain boy. Since this is the first time you had this type of "high" feeling, where your endorphins are exploding in your system, you want to keep experiencing it over and over again.

Maybe the first time you felt those electric feelings was when you were in a study group with smart, tall, and lanky Mike with his cool-looking glasses. Suddenly, Mike looked different to you. You noticed everything about him that you never paid attention to before. When he responded in kind, you were ecstatic. Your whole body seemed like it was electrically charged and that you were on the fastest roller coaster ride of your life. It felt fantastic!

Then you went to college and those smart, tall, lanky, glasses-wearing Mike types just did it for you all over again. The Mike type in the next cubicle in your office at your job may also elicit the same reaction from you. Unbeknownst to you, those early imprinted endorphin reactions that made you feel as though you were in ecstasy early on in your life are still working on you as an adult.

Equally, based on her early dating experiences and interactions with boys, a girl may be imprinted with the emotions—both positive and negative—that she felt during these formative dating years. That's why, in later years, it is not uncommon for adult women to seek out what feels familiar, even if that familiar feeling is a bad one.

Ever since the third grade, my client Ramona had a crush on Eric, the most popular boy in school. But Eric never paid her any attention. Her crush continued throughout high school, with Eric, now the star football player, still not paying her any mind. No matter how much she tried to get his attention, Eric was still not interested. So what happened to Ramona when she got older? She kept going after guys who were unattainable or not interested in her. She suffered a social life of heartbreak as she went through throngs of unattainable married men and men who weren't that into her who used her for sex and quickly dropped her.

Early Imprinting and Later Sexual Turn-ons

Just as women can be drawn to men who exhibit toxic behaviors they have observed early on in a parent, men can be drawn to specific toxic behaviors they learn early in life. For instance, if a man sees his father berating or beating his mother early in life, he may be imprinted or conditioned with this toxic behavior. So when he is older it may not be unusual for him to act the same way toward his significant other.

Sexual proclivities may be associated with imprinting as well. If a man has a specific sexual preference that you are not into and want him to stop doing, it may not be easy for him to stop if he has been imprinted with that particular sexual proclivity or fetish. Many sexual fetishes, proclivities, or turn-ons toward certain sexual behaviors begin to take root in childhood, prepuberty, or puberty. While not everyone who is exposed to certain experiences or materials develops a fetish, there are those who, for reasons based on their specific makeup, are more susceptible to it. But interviews with many who have certain fetishes show that there is a common denominator: they were imprinted with the experience at a very early age.

Imprinting Through Observing Others' Experiences

It's also possible to bear ill effects of an event that you witnessed during your formative years. Even if you were not in the middle of the action, if the incident was traumatic enough, it could cause a negative imprint that stays with you through adulthood.

For example, when my client Charlotte was eleven, she accidentally saw her father having sex with another woman. While riding her bicycle from a friend's house, she noticed a car on the side of the road that looked like her father's. She bicycled over to it and looked in the window, only to find her father in the back seat on top of a woman who was not her mother. Sick to her stomach and crying, she pedaled home as quickly as possible and told her mother what she had seen. The family soon broke up and her father never forgave her for "squealing" on him to her mother.

The effect this negative imprinting had on Charlotte was severe. When she grew up, she was extremely jealous and distrustful of men. She kept every boyfriend on a very short leash and watched every move they made like a hawk. If they dared speak to another woman in her presence, she went ballistic. She would constantly accuse them of having affairs, even if it was the last thing on the boy's mind. Needless to say, most of her boyfriends refused to put up with her "crazy" jealous behavior. So one after another, they dumped her.

Reversing the Imprint

Even though it is difficult to reverse imprinted behaviors and the mindset you developed in your formative years, it is not impossible. How do you do it?

The first step is to understand your imprints. Knowledge is power. When you have the knowledge that a pattern you are following began with your early boyfriends, then you have the power to consciously make a different choice. Think back to either of your parents' behavior when you were growing up. What actions did they model for you? Then think back to your early dating years. Were there any painful moments that could help explain your current behavior? It is essential that you get in touch with your own feelings. To jar your memory, look at photos of your past with your past boyfriends. Try to recall emotionally how you felt when you were with those boys or men in the photos.

Once you have this information, you can begin to try to consciously change your behavior so it's based on healthy choices, not negative imprinting. For example, here are some common behaviors based on negative imprints and their possible solutions.

Issue	Possible Solution
Chasing unavailable men	Date only men who approach you with genuine interest.
Getting involved with men who physically abuse you	Leave! You never have to put up with it.
Being unnecessarily jealous	Communicate and ask questions instead of assuming the worst.
Getting involved with men who cut you down or verbally abuse you	Speak up and put an immediate stop to it. Don't let anyone speak to you with disrespect.

For example, Ramona finally realized that her problems stemmed from her unrequited love of Eric. So she made a conscious decision to only respond to available men who made the first move, who showed initial interest in her, and who liked her for herself. She made the decision to respond to men whom she didn't have to go out of her way to impress. Incorporating her newfound knowledge into her life worked. Today, she is happily married to a devoted man who loves her.

Making these types of behavioral changes is very difficult. Remember, you are trying to change an imprint that could be decades old. Be patient with yourself and know that you will not be able to make a complete turnaround overnight. Just being aware of the fact is the first step in the right direction. Knowledge is definitely power. Now that you have the knowledge, you have the power to stop and re-evaluate your choices and your decisions. Changing your negative imprinting can help you break the cycle and allow you to welcome Nontoxic Men into your future. You'll now see the man for who he really is and not what your past or your early fantasies or imprinting made him out to be.

CHAPTER 6

Ten Reasons You May Be a Toxic Men Magnet

Top Ten "Toxic Men Magnet" Syndromes

I call women who keep choosing the same type of Toxic Man over and over again "Toxic Men magnets." There are ten major reasons why these women keep doing this over and over. They often suffer from one or more of the following ten Toxic Men Magnet Syndromes:

1. "Only I Can Tame the Bad Boy"
2. "My Love Is Like No Other"
3. "I Can Fix Anything and Anyone"
4. "Waiting for Prince Charming"
5. "Lonely Girl's Last Chance at Love"
6. "I Feel Sorry for Him"
7. "Not Trusting Initial Gut Reactions"
8. "Addicted to High Drama"
9. "Paralyzed by Fear"
10. "His Anger Shows Me He Really Cares"

Let's take a closer look at each syndrome to see if you could be suffering from one or more of them.

1. "Only I Can Tame the Bad Boy"

Women with this syndrome think they can be "the one" to finally tame the "bad boy" or change his toxic ways. This woman naively thinks that the bad boy or Toxic Man will eventually realize how special she is, a greater prize than any other woman, and that she is therefore worth changing his behavior for. Sadly, she is mistaken. It is her ego talking, not her rational mind. No matter how unique, beautiful, clever, or special this woman thinks she is—once a bad boy always a bad boy; she is never going to change him.

Women are duped into thinking that *their* behavior or actions will change a guy, when really only *he* can change his behavior and actions. Even if you cater to his every whim, look like Miss Universe, act like a porn star in the bedroom, and cook like a chef in a five-star restaurant, nothing will change or tame him. Too many women who correctly believe that they can change everything else in their lives wrongly believe that they can change a Toxic Man too. This is an illusion. You can never change anyone else, just as you cannot change the natural instincts of a wild animal. For example, some people raise wild tigers and leopards or gorillas. Even though they may be tame for a while, they are still wild animals with wild animal instincts. So why are their owners surprised when the wild animal for no reason at all mauls them?

Actor Charlie Sheen was dubbed one of Hollywood's Bad Boys. He got that reputation because of all the trouble he had with women. Most recently, he allegedly held a knife to his wife Brooke Mueller's throat, threatening to kill the mother of his then nine-month-old twin boys. He was arrested and subsequently freed on bail for a meager $850. Apparently Sheen also allegedly told his ex-wife, Denise Richards, while they were going through a divorce that he hoped she would die and threatened to have her, the mother of his two little girls, killed. Years earlier Sheen was on probation for assaulting girlfriend Brittany Ashland when she filed a lawsuit claiming he allegedly beat her up. Then there was yet another woman a year earlier, in 1995, whom Charlie allegedly beat up for not having sex with him. And finally in 1990, in an incident deemed an accident, he allegedly shot his then fiancée Kelly Preston, who is now actor John Travolta's wife. They broke up immediately after this incident.

Given his horrible history of alleged abusiveness toward women, why would anyone want to be with such a Toxic Man? Did his wealth, power, and fame blind these women, or did they think that they would be that special one who could tame him? The bottom line is that no woman can ever tame a man with a history of alleged abuse toward women. Significant behavior modification requires years of intensive therapy from a professional. Even then, there is no guarantee that a change in behavior will occur.

Women can't change a womanizer, either. Sanford was a very wealthy, classy, fifty-four-year-old bachelor who has never been faithful, from his first date at age sixteen throughout his three marriages. Then he met Candace, a wealthy forty-six-year-old widow who was convinced that she was the only woman in the world who could tame Sanford into a faithful husband. She thought her classiness, style, sensuality, sweetness, devotion, kindness, and generosity would be the magic ingredients that would make him never want to look at another woman again. She was wrong!

She *was* different from all his other wives, girlfriends, and lovers in that she kept quiet, tolerated his nasty personality quirks, bought him expensive gifts, catered to his every whim (both sexually and otherwise), and convinced him that he was the best lover since Casanova and that only he had the magical key to give her multiple (faked) orgasms. But although she finally manipulated him into marrying her, she could never manipulate him into not cheating on her. Her life was miserable. She constantly played detective, finding little papers with women's phone numbers, hotel receipts, lipstick- and makeup-stained clothes, perfume-infused sweaters, and even a pair of women's panties in his pants pocket. There was no way she would permanently stop Sanford's skirt-chasing.

2. "My Love Is Like No Other"

Other women believe that their love is so great that the Toxic Man has no choice but to change his bad ways. They, too, are mistaken. Any woman who believes that love will conquer all and that she will be the catalyst to change wayward or criminal behavior is grossly mistaken and extremely naive. Some women think that their feelings are deeper and stronger than other women's and that no one can reach the same depth of emotion that they feel for their man. Some women think they can love a man the way they love their child—unconditionally. But that is not the case with a man; a man has conditions. If he doesn't treat you right or he gets into trouble with the law, you can leave him, as you could not do with a child. Yet many women still attempt to achieve this unachievable emotional connection.

Kevin was a thief. He and a group of his cronies would steal jewelry, cash, stereos, and television sets from rich people's homes. When Sharon discovered how her boyfriend earned a living, she pleaded with him to stop, but he refused. She stayed with him anyway. She told him that her love for him was so great, she would work ten jobs if need be, if he would just stop burglarizing homes. She told him that she loved him unconditionally and that her life was devoted to him. Touched by Sharon's love and devotion, Kevin told her that he would stop hanging out with his cronies and quit stealing.

Making good on her word, she worked several jobs and gave Kevin all of her earnings. He appeared to have stopped the thievery. She was convinced it was her immense love and devotion for Kevin that made him quit his wayward behavior. But then Kevin was caught burglarizing someone's home and was arrested. No love, no matter how deep, could make Kevin stop his criminal behavior.

3. "I Can Fix Anything and Anyone"

There is another group of women who try to fix men: the changers. They are usually high-powered, successful women who have moved mountains in their professional life and think they can do the same in their personal life. Therapists, psychologists, doctors, social workers, and counselors often fall prey to this syndrome. After all, they make their living fixing people, so they think it can work in their personal relationships as well. They are mistaken. You can only fix someone in your personal life if they want to be fixed, not if you want them fixed.

These women have the same mentality as Kendra, who was president of a major company. She had a history of success in accomplishing the impossible. Overcoming extreme poverty and living in a car with her homeless mother for most of her early childhood, she finally grew up to live the American dream. She graduated from Harvard Business School, moved up the corporate ladder to become not only a multimillionaire, but a "mover and a shaker" and a major international policymaker. In her professional life, she did the impossible. She thought she could do the same in her personal life.

While walking along the boardwalk in Venice Beach, California, she spotted a tall, lanky "starving artist"–type painting a seascape. After a brief chat, she said she was looking for some paintings for her office and asked to see some of his other paintings in his studio. She quickly learned that his studio was the open air of Venice Beach and that he didn't know where his other paintings were scattered because he lived on various friends' couches.

While talking to him, Kendra noticed underneath his slovenly appearance—his greasy long hair, scraggly beard, and unkempt clothes—was a really cute guy with beautiful green eyes and a gorgeous smile, despite his discolored teeth. It was then that she decided that he would be her next project. She would change his living situation and his looks, make him her boyfriend, her fiancé, and eventually her husband, whom she would transform into a successful artist. She fantasized about having exhibitions for him and getting him an art gallery. She decided that this man was just what she needed, a creative artist type to balance out her image.

As time passed, she failed to see the fruits of her labor. Even though he had a studio and paints and supplies, Ted was not doing much painting. In fact, he was not doing much of anything except getting high on pot.

After being gone for a week, she came home to find the same Ted she saw on the Venice boardwalk—unkempt and slovenly and getting high on her expensive leather couch and mashing the ashes from his joint into the expensive Lalique dish on her coffee table. Kendra told Ted to leave her home immediately.

Ted was exactly who he was when she first met him—a very laid-back guy, more interested in getting high and hanging out with his buddies than he was in building a career as an artist. He wasn't going to change no matter how much Kendra tried to change him.

4. "Waiting for Prince Charming"

This syndrome highlights the power of imprinting. It is based on how little girls have been conditioned throughout their childhoods with stories of Cinderella, Snow White, and Sleeping Beauty. Each of these characters is rescued by Prince Charming and, as a result, ends up living "happily ever after." Prince Charming seems to show up in every single fairy tale that caters to little girls. He shows up in Snow White, Sleeping Beauty, Cinderella, and the Frog Prince. Written in the 1800s, these stories are simply not relevant in today's world. In the early days, especially in Europe where these stories were first created, women didn't have many rights and little girls certainly did not have many dreams, with the exception of finding a man who would determine their fate in life.

No little girl in any part of the world should ever be taught that her fate, her future, and her worth depends on finding any man, no matter how handsome or charming the prince may be. Unfortunately, these imprinted myths have remained in the minds of too many grown women, who still believe in the notion that there is a Prince Charming out there waiting to rescue and take care of them.

Why not think of yourself as a young princess making it on your own, or helping others to make it? How about learning that the damsel never needs to be in distress or to be rescued or enabled by anyone? Why not tell yourself that you're a strong, capable woman instead of a victim in distress? Why not remind yourself that beauty is not on the outside (such as in the form of a beautiful gown and crown), but that beauty is on the inside? Why not remember that it's good deeds, abilities, and being kind and loving to others that makes you a beautiful princess?

If you think I am being harsh, you are correct; I am. Unfortunately, I have witnessed generations of women still living with the illusion imprinted into their brain that there would indeed be that one special Prince Charming who will be there to save them and make their lives perfect, so that they can live "happily ever after." What happens to these little girls who grow up searching their whole lives for Prince Charming or someone like him to rescue them? When they find out he was just an illusion—a myth—they often become bitter and angry. Others become insecure and suffer from low self-esteem. They feel inadequate because they weren't able to secure a real-life version of the illusion they tucked away in the recesses of their developing minds.

Women cannot believe that another person will always be there to rescue them. It is not only irresponsible, it is dangerous. This notion is damaging to women in that it psychologically infantilizes them, affecting their self-esteem and independence. Too many women have been conditioned to think of themselves as a failure if they have not found their Prince Charming. Their self-worth depends not only on their being married, but on their being married to a certain kind of man. That is why so many women are willing to put up with a man's toxicity because he has money, position, or power to take care of them. But the reality is that the price of being rescued and taken care of is often too high.

It's only a myth that a man will do it all for you, as Linda discovered. Bill, twenty years her senior, wined and dined her, bought her expensive gifts, took her on exotic vacations, paid off her large credit card debts, and even gave her a cash allowance along with his black American Express card to use as she desired. She married him because she thought she would have it made for the rest of her life. She was mistaken! There was huge price for her to pay for being "taken care of" and "rescued." At his whim, she had to accompany Bill on all his business trips and events where a spouse (especially a sexy beautiful young spouse to create envy among his peers) was a standard requirement. She had to be available for dinner outings with him where he entertained associates. He told her how to dress, what to eat, how to wear her hair, what to read, and which shows she could watch.

Getting your hair and nails done at the best salons, spending the day at the gym or the masseuse, and shopping with someone else's credit card may seem fun, but a steady diet of it gets old. When Linda had to be at Bill's beck and call, she was not able to hang out with friends, wear, say, or eat what she wanted, or even sleep when she wanted. Life was not good. Add to that a bad sex life because Bill was impotent and too selfish to please her, and life got even worse. To top it off, Bill made her the butt of his jokes, and spoke condescendingly to her.

One day Linda told Bill that she wanted to take acting classes and become an actress. He dismissed her idea as being ridiculous and forbade her to do it. She did it anyway and they finally divorced. Even though she is now a struggling actress who lives maidless in a one-bedroom apartment, she is thrilled. She has her freedom.

5. "Lonely Girl's Last Chance at Love"

Too many women are so desperate for a man that they will, unfortunately, put up with anything to have a man, even if he is toxic. It's not enough to simply be grateful that at least you are finally with a man who wants to sleep with you, live with you, and have children with you. Unfortunately, a plethora of lonely women with low self-worth will put up with emotional and/or physical torture by remaining in toxic relationships, just to have a man in their life.

There are too many women, obviously lacking self-esteem, who fall into this syndrome. They feel it is better to have somebody, no matter how bad or toxic, than to have no one. They believe that since it took so long to find a man, they will never find another one again. They have convinced themselves that this is as good as it gets. That is why they stay in the relationship for too long (or never leave!), no matter how miserable the relationship. Unfortunately, these women are stuck in the hell of being with a Toxic Man because of their lack of self-esteem. By remaining with them, they will never know that there can be a healthy, happy relationship with someone else.

To avoid this syndrome, take a better look at yourself and realize that no man is worth being treated badly. If you could have a relationship with a man even after not having one for such a long period of time, know that you can have another one as well. This isn't the last man in the world for you. There are plenty of others who will appreciate you and treat you with the respect you deserve.

For example, Marie thought she had better stay put with her Toxic Man because that was all she'd ever get. She had not dated for ten years, since she was in college. She tried everything in those ten years to find a man—online dating, singles cruises, matchmakers, singles ads, singles dances, and fixups. She hated being lonely, going to movies alone, traveling alone, going out to dinner alone—and most of all, sleeping alone.

She finally met Gary, a slacker, whose girlfriend kicked him out because she was sick of him mooching off of her, not contributing to the relationship, and spending his days skateboarding and playing games online. But that is not what he told Marie when he met her. He gave her a sob story about how mean his ex-girlfriend was and how she kicked him out with just his skateboard and the clothes on his back. Being desperate, he smelled Marie's desperation as well. Marie was so anxious for a man in her life that she immediately invited him to move in with her.

Thrilled to have a man after a decade, she quickly realized why his ex-girlfriend kicked him out. He mooched off her, skateboarded all day, never looked for a job, never had any money, and, worst of all, never bathed, which pretty much killed their sex life. She hated sleeping with him, let alone having sex with him. But she kept him anyway. She thought her choice was having a Toxic Man or no man. She chose the Toxic Man, and remains with this stinky moocher to this day.

6. "I Feel Sorry for Him"

Because most women tend to be nurturers, it is easy for them to become prey to a Toxic Man who is looking to use them for sex, a place to live, or financial gain. The trick of this toxic con artist is to tell you one woe after another until he taps into something that strikes you emotionally. He watches your body language like a hawk until he sees that you are falling for his story. Then he elaborates. He gets more dramatic with each word, telling his story in such a way that there is no option but to feel sorry for him. The urgency in his voice is manipulated to let you know that he is stuck and there is no way out, unless you come to his rescue.

Most of these Toxic Men want money or sex. Giving any money to a man under any circumstances is unacceptable, especially in the courting stages. While it may keep him there for a while, it definitely won't last. He'll take your money, but he usually won't take you in the long run. Never fall for his challenge to be the one who rescues him from of his lack-of-sex or lack-of-money problem. That is not your responsibility—and, ironically, it will only cause him to disrespect you for being dumb enough to fall for his con.

A married Toxic Man who wants to use a woman for sex typically tells her that his wife refuses to have sex with him and he hasn't had sex in five years. He says it using a devastated and sad tone, telling his prey that he is depressed and plans to leave his wife, but he's torn. He says he is loyal, has never cheated on his wife, and/or is a religious guy who loves his kids but he can't go on like this any longer. He says that more than anything, he wants to find a loving woman who really understands him. When he does find her, he will be out of the house for good. He will be ready to start his new life with his new, understanding, and nurturing wife.

In essence, he is offering up a challenge to which many women would be receptive. Be a nurturing, loving girlfriend (with sex being part of that nurturing). Then I will see how much more loving you are than my wife, so I can leave her and marry you. But it is a sham. He has no intention of leaving his wife. His only intention is to have sex with you. Avoid these Toxic Men at all costs.

In essence, this type of Toxic Man tests you. He lets you know the urgency of the situation and how he needs help. He leaves it up to you to make the next move. If you make the next move, he has a new sex partner. And you think you're his future wife. Unfortunately, that is never the case with these predatory Toxic Men.

Besides sex, money is the motivation behind a Toxic Man's con to make you feel sorry for him and be his savior. This is what happened to Annette. She met Glenn on an Internet dating site. Soon into their relationship, Glenn put on a dour expression, waiting for Annette to make the first move and ask what was wrong.

Cleverly, he said he had issues but didn't want to burden her with them. She insisted they speak about it. That was the first good sign, he thought. He paused at first to feign holding back, and then let loose with a torrent of problems from losing money in the market, to his ex-wife taking him to court for more child support, to his son needing an operation and not have enough money to help him because he couldn't afford health insurance. It was then he noticed Annette's concerned look. Now he had her hooked into his dilemma. Then he continued with this finale—needing money to pay this month's rent or he would be evicted. With each problem, his voice got more and more desperate, indicating the urgency of his plight in his quest for squeezing money out of his prey.

When Annette reacted with, "You won't have a place to live!" Glenn knew that he had her just where he wanted her. Stupidly, because she felt sorry for him, she agreed to give him a money order for $5,000. He took the money and ran, never to be heard from again.

7. "Not Trusting Initial Gut Reactions"

If your intuition tells you that something is not right, pay attention to it. You are always right. It is your body giving you a warning signal that something is wrong. Often, your intuition will come in the form of an anxiety-provoking feeling. You may feel on edge or restless. Your stomach may even cramp up or your head will start to hurt. You may even feel that your heart is beating faster, and not in a good way. Your face is tense and often topped by a furrowed brow. You may even find it difficult to sleep or eat, or, on the other hand, you may find that you are suddenly eating or drinking too much or eating the wrong things (such as comfort food because you feel so anxious). Don't ignore these signals. They are telling you that there is something wrong. This is your warning sign to open your eyes and your ears so that you can see and hear who the man really is.

As soon as Gloria met Larry at the cocktail party it was "hate at first sight." For some reason unknown to her, she detested him. Whether it was his walk, leer, or tight smile, something about Larry turned her off. After following her around the party all night, he somehow managed to find out her name and where she worked. The next day, he looked her up online and phoned her to have lunch. She didn't want to go, but thought that since he went to the trouble of finding her number, what harm could a simple lunch do? Somehow at lunch, he managed to finagle his way into a formal date with her, then to a museum to see an exhibit by her favorite artist, then to a concert to hear her favorite group, and then to a surprise dinner with her favorite wine and a gift—a scarf by her favorite designer in her favorite color. He learned all this information about her from her Facebook page.

Now she was hooked. She brushed off her initial negative reaction toward him and began a full-blown relationship, moving into his beautiful condo. Months into the relationship, all of his "thoughtfulness" became more and more annoying. He bought her new clothes, made hairdresser appointments for her to get a new hairstyle, got her a gym membership, where he insisted they both go to work out each morning. She finally figured out that Larry was a total control freak, who not only tried to change everything about her but started to control with whom she spoke and with whom she could be friends. The ten calls a day when he was at work or when she was out and about were no longer flattering. They were disturbing.

She had enough of him and moved out. But before she did, she left a note on his bed along with the cell phone he bought her. It said, "I should have listened to my initial gut instinct about you—you're creepy. Don't call me or contact me ever again." Being the control freak that he was, Larry did not heed Gloria's warning until she got a restraining order against him, which he violated, sending him to jail.

The moral of this story is that if your initial feeling is that something is wrong, you are absolutely right. Don't second-guess yourself.

8. "Addicted to High Drama"

Countless women knowingly or unknowingly put themselves in positions where they are exposed to unstable, violent men simply for the sake of drama. For them, it is like being in a real-life action movie where there is danger and the possibility that they may not survive. While it may be thrilling for the moment, this high-drama addiction to the wrong man is no movie and no game. It is serious and can even cost you your life.

Many women seek the dramatic thrill because there is something missing in their lives. They may even walk around feeling nothing but boredom. The thrill of danger makes their endorphins flow. It makes them feel alive. They mistake the red-alert feeling of danger for excitement and happiness. As a result, they get themselves into serious trouble. The fact that they are the central figure in this dangerous equation adds to their excitement. They find it thrilling that their presence can elicit such an over-the-top reaction from a man.

Yet too many women mistake this reaction for love and a feeling that someone cares about them. Why else, they think, would a man act so emotionally or violently toward a woman if he didn't have intense feelings toward her? But these women are severely misguided. A man's violence toward you is not the measure of how strongly he feels about you or how much he loves you. It is the complete opposite. Thrill-seeking women are playing with fire. It is a deadly game and they will never win. Love is never violent, and the thrill they feel is in reality their instincts telling them that something is very wrong.

Christina, an extreme sufferer of this high-drama syndrome, has been yelled at, cursed at, pushed out of a moving car, purposely locked out of her own apartment, driven around while hanging onto a hood of a car, choked and almost strangled, given a split lower lip and a broken nose, pushed down a flight of stairs, held with a gun at her head, locked in a closet, and made to walk home alone at two in the morning without wearing a stitch of clothing.

No, Christina is not an actress in a soap opera. She is a woman who gets into repeated toxic situations with one Toxic Man after another. She is addicted to the high drama that often comes with being with a Toxic Man. Christina describes herself as a victim; she tells me she has no clue how she ends up with these Toxic Men. But in reality, she gets some sort of sick pleasure from this high drama. She has experienced it with her two ex-husbands and the myriad of toxic boyfriends she draws in like a magnet. Her acceptance of these horrible behaviors from the men in her life is no doubt due to a very low sense of self-worth. In Christina's mind, this is all she thinks she deserves. Unfortunately, early on in her developmental history with men, she has learned to mistakenly equate abuse from men as a sign of their love and caring about her.

9. "Paralyzed by Fear"

One of the main reasons women become Toxic Men magnets is because of fear and intimidation. If they are confronted with an overly persistent man, they are innately afraid of what will happen if they don't do what that man says. Even if they don't want to do it, they oblige. These women live in fear—fear of not being liked, fear of not hurting anyone's feelings. With little or no regard to their own feelings, they end up severely hurting themselves. They don't know how to speak up, say no, and mean it.

Because they don't know how to stick up for themselves, they often turn a blind eye to a man's toxic behavior. This further diminishes their already low self-esteem because they are upset at themselves for continuing to accept his behavior. Because of their fear of fighting back and sticking up for themselves, these emotional doormats are significant targets for the Toxic Man's cycle of abuse.

If these women are abused long enough, they will often develop a numbness, not only toward the abuse but to everything else going on around them. Why? This is caused by the overproduction of certain chemicals in the brain that block sensation during extreme stress. So when there is a prolonged period of fear due to prolonged emotional abuse and trauma, the body produces opiates, which produce both emotional and physical numbness, thereby affecting the ability to think and act clearly.

Most of us are familiar with Stockholm syndrome, where the abused victim has positive feelings of adulation toward or identifies with his or her abuser, out of extreme fear. The victim ends up numbly complying with everything the abuser says. Essentially, the same thing occurs in situations when a woman is emotionally, mentally, and physically abused over time. As a result of her extreme fear, she becomes numb to her environment and what is really going on around her.

The photo of successful children's book author Hedda Nussbaum with her bruised face and flattened nose is the indelible picture sketched in the minds of anyone who remembers her horrific nightmare from the late 1980s. While it may be an extreme case, her story of domestic abuse clearly illustrates how prolonged fear can allow a woman to remain in a toxic situation. Repeatedly brutalized, she got to the point where she became so anesthetized, she didn't intercede when something so horrific as child abuse and the subsequent brutal murder of her six-year-old adopted daughter occurred. The only positive thing that came out of this case is that after repeated plastic surgeries to repair the permanent damage from Joel's hands and years of intense counseling, Hedda Nussbaum has dedicated her life to helping battered women and lectures to women across the country about the subject of abuse.

While many cases may not be as extreme as Hedda's, many women's emotional numbness to their continued abuse is the reason they stay in an abusive relationship for way too long. This is why it is essential to have a support team of people around you who love you and can help you "wake up" from the constant abuse so that you can finally leave.

10. "His Anger Shows Me He Really Cares"

In a good mood and doing one of the things I love most, shoe shopping, my mood quickly soured as I heard an "oldie but goodie" song playing over the store's sound system. My jaw dropped to the ground as I listened to the words of this catchy tune, "He hit me and it felt like a kiss." I immediately typed those lyrics into my iPhone to see who in their right mind would write, record, or produce a song with such egregious lyrics. When I discovered that Phil Spector, the infamous music producer, was involved with this 1962 song, I wasn't surprised. This is the same man who is now in prison for killing actress Lana Clarkson. He is the same man who allegedly used to abuse women and literally put a gun to their heads.

Unfortunately, many women equate physical violence from a man with the warped thinking that the man must love them very much, otherwise he wouldn't care enough to hit them.

If a man hits you or threatens to kill you, it means he doesn't care about you. It's not cute and it is not flattering. It means that he is out of control and doesn't respect you. If he doesn't respect you, he clearly doesn't love you, because the definition of love is respect and admiration. Moreover, it means that he is a highly disturbed individual and a danger to you.

You must have zero tolerance for any man who hits you under any circumstance.

Although a man's use of physical violence when angry may result from imprinting—such as if his parent hit or spanked him and afterward said, "I spanked you for your own good," "I spanked you because I love you," or "I spanked you because I care about you"—it is wrong and twisted thinking.

This type of misguided thinking is unacceptable. If a man hits you, it does not mean that he cares about you and loves you. It means that he does *not* love you. You must never accept this treatment. You need to extract yourself from that relationship and never look back. Don't delude yourself into thinking that he is going to change or that it won't happen again. Rest assured that it will happen again, only the next time it may be even more brutal. Brutality is not love. Love is not supposed to hurt and give you pain. This is why you need the support of level-headed people who can teach you that this abuse is not normal behavior from a man and should not be tolerated. If you don't have such people in your life, find a woman's domestic abuse support group and attend a meeting. This will give you an immediate reality check.

Establish Boundaries in Your Relationships

One thing all of these "syndromes" have in common is that the woman is in some way allowing the Toxic Man to run the relationship and call the shots. That's why it's so important to maintain your own identity, friendships with loved ones, and goals in a relationship. One way to do that is to clearly establish certain boundaries, and then be consistent in monitoring them. You must set limits as to what you will and will not accept. Don't bend to his wishes just to keep your man happy, while your own needs aren't met. This type of relationship will never work in the long run.

Let's say you want to hang out with your mother or your girlfriends and your man sulks or tells you he doesn't want you to go. Let him know that your relationship with your mother or best friend is non-negotiable. Let him know that your love for him has nothing to do with your feelings toward those who are close to you. If he insists you not go, then he is showing signals of being a Toxic Man whose aim is to control you. Don't let him guilt you into feeling bad about going. He needs to know early on that this is who you are and that he must respect who and what is important to you. In the long run, he will respect you for it.

CHAPTER 7

How a Toxic Man Ensnares His Victims

Damsels in Distress Are Prey for Any Toxic Man

How many women grow up playing the "I'm dumb. Help me!" act? Whether they are blonde, brunette, or redhead, these women have been raised to believe that being a "damsel in distress" has worked for other females (e.g., Snow White, Sleeping Beauty, and Cinderella, as we discussed in Chapter 6). So why can't it work for them?

In the days of chivalry and chauvinism, the damsel in distress act may have worked for the majority of women because most men believed that women were the weaker sex and needed men's help to function in the world. But since women are no longer the helpless sex of yesteryear, with women equaling or surpassing almost any male achievement, it is a lot more difficult to get a man—especially an evolved and emotionally healthy one—to rescue or save you.

In some cases, you are not even looking for a man to rescue you from your troubles, when suddenly there he is. Almost out of nowhere, he shows up in your life, like a shark drawn to blood. He's a sharp and clever Toxic Man. He is quickly able to read what's ailing you. Perhaps it is your broken heart from a past boyfriend, the death of a family member or pet, recovering from or dealing with an illness, not getting that promotion, or getting laid off. Perhaps he reads your insecurity and lack of confidence due to a weight gain, or perceives that your last birthday has left you feeling not so young and pretty anymore. If he spots these signs, a Toxic Man will know just how to pique your interest. . . .

The Toxic Man Knows How to Reel You In

A Toxic Man knows exactly what to do and say in order to reel you in like a trout out of a lake. He will do whatever it takes to gain your confidence in him. He may spend hours listening to your woes and offer up suggestions as to how he can help, and even do some things to actually make your predicament a lot better. You can't believe your good fortune. "The tide has finally changed," you think. "What a great guy! This man is like an angel from heaven."

In actuality, he's not the great guy he has led you to believe. He is no angel from heaven, but rather a devil from hell, which you will eventually discover. He is only there to help you so that he can help himself. Following are some of the motivations a Toxic Man may have for being so nice to you up front.

HE IS TRYING TO BUILD UP HIS OWN EGO

You may be the vehicle that the Toxic Man uses in order to help him build up his damaged ego. A Toxic Man cannot accept defeat. If a past woman in his life left him standing there like an idiot, his ego will need a boost. Maybe she said he wasn't her type. Or perhaps she abruptly left him for a handsomer, wealthier, and younger man. Maybe his ego couldn't take it, and he thought that he'd be damned if he would allow anyone to reject him. So to gain control of the situation, he searched high and low to find that same woman who left him standing there. Then he seduced her again and told her that he couldn't live without her, so she would be so flattered and agree to get involved in a relationship with him again, so he could restore his bruised and fragile ego.

HE IS TRYING TO MAKE A BUCK OFF YOU

The Toxic Man may want you around because you are the key to giving him something he could never get on his own. He tries to exercise control over you so he can ride your gravy train and leech off of your achievements—your work and effort and, subsequently, the rewards. He is after the spoils that come in the form of undeserved credit, money, or both.

HE WANTS TO TAKE OUT HIS INNER ISSUES ON YOU

You may be the perfect emotional punching bag for the ...,
whereby he takes out on you the aggression and hatred he feels toward
women in his past who have done him wrong. If a Toxic Man has just
been dumped, he may reflect his abandonment issues on you, his next
victim. Or, perhaps his mother abandoned him—either literally, giving
him up for adoption, or more loosely, by not paying enough attention
to him when he was young. At any rate, he was not going to let another
woman get away with abandoning him.

The more weak, vulnerable, insecure, and emotional a woman gets,
often the crueler and more hostile the Toxic Man gets. It's because he feels
he has the power to lord over his subject. This kind of Toxic Man may
even get physically violent with you. He loves the position in which he
has put you. He's controlling the puppet strings by what he says and does,
and in how you react. Your weakness and emotional dependence on him
give him a false sense of strength. The truth is that although he may be
in a position of power, deep down he is not strong, but rather weak and
fragile. He is hiding behind a position of power because in reality he has
no real power of his own, as he doesn't face his issues head-on.

The moral of the story is that often if you don't do exactly what the
Toxic Man wants you to do, his deep-rooted anger (which usually has
nothing to do with you) will undoubtedly surface. If he tries to control
your life and you don't do what he says, he often becomes out of control
and lashes out—even physically.

If a Man Sounds Too Good to Be True, He Is!

When you are in a vulnerable place in your life, your judgment is skewed.
Through vulnerable eyes, every man may look like Prince Charming to
you, when in reality he may be nothing more than a Toxic Man.

Think back to the Cinderella fairy tale again. Cinderella was indeed
vulnerable. After all, her mother died when she was very young and her
father was nowhere to be seen. Thus, she was left with a mean stepmother

with mean daughters to abuse her. She was essentially their maid, cooking and cleaning up after them, while they frolicked and partied. In Cinderella's mind, any man who took her away from this dreary existence would be a prince. Yet a real Prince Charming came to rescue her from a life of hurt, loneliness, and tears. So when he immediately asked her to marry him, without hesitation, Cinderella said "Yes!"

Like Cinderella, too many women have said an impetuous Yes to a marriage proposal made by their perceived Prince Charming. They anxiously jump at the chance. After all, he swept them off their feet and is now willing to rescue them from a life of hurt, loneliness, and tears. It seems too good to be true. They get caught up in the excitement of it all. "It's like a dream. It's too good to be true," they think. "I better hurry up and say yes before he changes his mind."

But unfortunately, for too many women this dream quickly turns into a nightmare because it definitely was too good to be true. In fact, it wasn't true at all. Had they taken more time and done diligence, they would have discovered that their mythical Prince was actually a Toxic Man. They would have clearly seen that their quick wedding was a sham, and they would not live "happily ever after."

Look for These Signs

Depending on which type of Toxic Man you encounter, he may use different techniques to make you his next victim. Here's a quick list of what to look for in each Toxic Type:

1. The **Jealous Competitor** will let you know that he is jealous only because of his intense love for you. He will let you know that his competitive spirit with you is meant to keep you on your toes so that you can always strive to be the best you can be.

2. The **Sneaky Passive-Aggressive Silent-but-Deadly Erupting Volcano** will attract you by always being pleasant and on even keel. Even when things call for being upset, he will never show it, as he always wants you to see him as "Mr. Nice Guy."

3. The **Arrogant Self-Righteous Know-It-All** will attract you by going out of his way to give you helpful information. Whether it is in the form of documents, a link, an article, or a book, he will make sure that he is your information source. He will also connect you with the "right" people who may help you—such as doctors or lawyers—in order to show you not only how much he knows but who he knows. He is always there to help you solve any problem and give you advice.

4. The **Seductive Manipulative Cheating Liar** will ensnare you with his gift of gab and seductive tones. He will have believable excuses and the well-thought-out stories that you want to believe. He is also very sensuous and giving sexually, as well as generous with gifts and surprises. He is a lot of fun to be around and generates excitement as he sweeps you off your feet. He will often do spur-of-the-moment extravagant things to impress you, such as taking you to exotic places.

5. The **Angry Bullying Control Freak** will lure you through his take-charge approach; he will let you know that you never have to worry about anything else again. He is there to rescue you from everything. He is very generous in that he will readily buy you a new wardrobe—or a breast enlargement—but is the gifts are meant to keep you dependent on him financially. Since he needs to control, he also needs to tell you how to look, and if he doesn't like the way you dress or the shape of your body, he will pay to do something about it.

6. The **Instigating Backstabbing Meddler** will attract you by getting involved in your business. He will make phone calls on your behalf or introduce you to people he thinks could help you in business or personally. He may even help facilitate reconciliations with your family members. If you and a friend have had a falling out or you haven't seen a friend or a relative in a while, he may initiate a call to make the reconnection between you two. Since he thrives on getting involved, he will usually create the interactions with you and others. It may also be banal: if you complain that you don't like your unreliable

vacuum cleaner, he will get you the newest state-of-the-art kind. He listens to your every need and makes sure it is met.

7. The **Self-Destructive Gloom-and-Doom Victim** will try to ensnare you by making you feel sorry for him. He will sing his woes and wait for you to be the one to jump in to bail him out. When you do help, he will show eternal gratitude. He will sing your praises and let you know that there was no way he could have made it without you. He never lets you forget that you are his savior.

8. The **Wishy-Washy Spineless Wimp** will attract you by being overly accommodating—he will let you make all the decisions and he will never make waves. He will gladly go along with whatever you do and say. This makes you think he is an excellent companion because he is so easy to be around; he lets you be you.

9. The **Selfish Me-Myself-and-I Narcissist** will lure you by letting you know that there is no one better than him for you (as he shows you how lucky you are to have him). He will often shower you with extraordinary, unique, and often over-the-top gifts and tell you what lengths he went to in order to get you these gifts. He wants you to appreciate him and his great efforts. Because he is so concerned with his own looks and how he appears to others, he is equally concerned with your looks. He will encourage you to get plastic surgery because you will look better on his arm. You may even be flattered as he encourages you to dress in a certain style to look more sexy or more classy. But it is ultimately done with him in mind, as he wants you to look good because he sees you as an appendage of him.

10. The **Emotional Refrigerator** will attract you with his aloofness. He will pose himself as a challenge to you. He won't always be emotionally unavailable. But in order to attract you, he will occasionally get out of character. From time to time, he may show you a hot, passionate side of himself that will intrigue you. Because he does it occasionally, you are always waiting for his passion to surface again. In essence, this "operant conditioning" technique is what keeps you around.

11. The **Socio-Psychopath** will attract you by doing and saying anything he thinks you would want to hear. If he know you like a certain food or jewelry, he will make sure you get it. He will discover your vulnerable, emotional spots and play to them. He will make you feel as though he is the only one who really understands you, which makes you stay connected to him.

Toxic Men are often quite proficient at these tactics—that's why women fall for them again and again! They are very convincing. That's why knowing what to look for at the outset of your future relationships will help you avoid being ensnared in the first place.

PART III

Sizing Up a Toxic Man

CHAPTER 8

Trust Your Gut

Never Ignore the Signs

Here are five simple questions I want you to answer.

1. Do you listen to that little voice in you that screams NO! NO! NO!?
2. Do you respond to that knot in your stomach that tells you that something isn't right?
3. Do you pay close attention and listen to the exact words someone says, instead of editing his words in your mind and giving his message the meaning you want to hear?
4. Do you often ignore someone's gruff tone of voice, and instead make excuses for him such as "He was probably having a bad day" or "He didn't mean to sound annoyed with me"?
5. Do you watch someone's face like a hawk, so you can see the exact nuances on his face, that reflect how he really feel about you?

If your answers indicate that you ignore your gut, don't watch body and facial language, and make excuses for others, it is because you, like many of us, are in denial when it comes to both hearing and seeing the truth about another person.

Ever since grade school, many of us have been falsely brainwashed that we are all supposed to get along and love everyone and everyone is supposed to love us. But this isn't reality. The truth is that you won't love everyone and everyone won't love you. There will be people to whom you are toxic, just as there will be people who are toxic to you. Some people will be friends while others will be foes. In order to save yourself grief, time, and effort, it is important that you quickly learn how to discern friends from foes or the toxic from the nontoxic. The only way you can accomplish this is by doing three things. They are:

1. Opening your eyes and really looking at what you see;
2. Opening your ears and really listening to what you hear;
3. Trusting the feelings you feel that are based on everything you just saw and heard.

Doing all of the above is called "trusting your instincts." Even if you don't like what you saw or heard and wish you saw or heard something else, you have to accept it as gospel truth.

Animal Survival Depends on Trusting Instincts—Yours Does Too!

In Chapter 1, I mentioned that deep in the brain there is a limbic system that gets you in touch with your emotions. You must always listen to these emotions, because they are always correct in terms of how you really feel about someone.

Animals are very attuned to trusting their instincts—their very survival depends on it. They can quickly ascertain who is friend or foe and whom they like and whom they don't like, in a matter of milliseconds. Whenever I would walk my Lhasa apso, Lambear, on the streets of New York, I was continually amazed at how he would wag his tail and insist on playing with certain dogs, bare his teeth and growl at other dogs, and completely ignore other dogs. Lambear immediately knew whom he liked and whom he didn't like. There were no social pretenses. Unlike many of us, he didn't care what anyone else thought about his decision, or if the dogs whom he ignored or didn't like had hurt feelings. He didn't feel guilty about liking certain dogs or disliking others.

The anger he displayed by his sharp barks, growls, and baring of teeth may have saved his life on many occasions, avoiding unnecessary doggie brawls. His body language signs told other dogs he felt were toxic to him:

"I'm on to you and I don't like you. Don't even think about messing with me." Perhaps if you listened to your own instincts, as revealed through your limbic system, you too could save yourself a lot of grief, especially when it comes to dealing with Toxic Men in your life.

Consequences of Ignoring Your Instincts in Business

Many women who have to face Toxic Men in the business world often turn their pain and anger inward. Not knowing how to deal with the toxicity hurled at them, they end up feeling stuck and helpless.

This is especially true if the woman isn't very sure of herself, isn't knowledgeable about certain areas, or relies on professional advice. Most people work with professionals based on recommendations from friends and family or other professionals whom they respect, but on some level, it doesn't matter what praises anyone bestows on another person. It doesn't matter whether he is a doctor, lawyer, or chief executive officer. It's completely up to you to pay careful attention to any signals or signs that don't feel right and act upon them.

Whether or not you are a woman with a career, you have to be alert for things that do not sound, look, or seem right to you. You have to carefully listen to what people say and be on the lookout for consistencies. Do this person's words sync up with his body language and facial expressions? After saying something in the affirmative, does he shake his head to signal "no" when he should be nodding it "yes"? Does he look away or lean away from you when speaking? These are just a few things to pay attention to. If something doesn't ring true or you feel that something is off balance, trust your instincts. You are usually right.

One widow who continued to invest her money with now-jailed Ponzi schemer Bernie Madoff devalued her gut instincts when she first met him. She had never met Madoff when her husband was alive; he had taken care of their finances. But when she had her first meeting with Madoff, after her husband's death, she felt there was something strange about him. She thought he was condescending and felt a detachedness about him. She shared her feelings with family members, who dismissed them as her being in grieving mode. Relatives reiterated that Madoff was the best, and there were no other options. Reluctantly and unfortunately, she listened to her relatives. Not acting on the toxic signals she picked up from Bernie Madoff cost her a fortune.

Consequences of Ignoring Your Instincts on a Personal Level

Second-guessing your instincts when dealing with a professional in an industry you're not familiar with (say, your accountant) can be understandable. That is why it is so important to ask questions until you feel comfortable with the person who is handling your financial, medical, or legal needs. But when you are dealing with a potential partner in your personal life, you must never ignore your gut. When two people are looking for love, neither has the upper hand. Since a personal relationship is almost entirely based on feelings and emotions, it is essential for you to pay very close attention to what is being said, how it is being said, and whether the body and facial language match what is being said. If something doesn't sound right or look right, don't ignore your instincts or sweep them under the rug—you will be doing yourself a lot of harm in the long run.

Forget about political correctness or thinking that you may be judging a person too quickly or too harshly if you trust your instincts. If someone does or says something that doesn't feel right to you, pay attention and ask questions to make sure you understand exactly what he meant to say. Doing so helps confirm your initial instinct. On the other hand, asking questions can clarify something you may perhaps have misunderstood. But if there has been no misunderstanding and what he said or how he behaved turned you off, trust your instincts.

Know That You Know What You Know

Here's the simple truth about the best way to avoid involvement with a Toxic Man: never ignore warning signs. I've found that most Toxic Men will give off some signs that they are toxic during your first meeting or conversation. That's why it's so important to be vigilant about watching for the signs and then acting on them by not continuing to allow this Toxic Man in your life. Granted, some men are better than others at hiding their toxic traits, but trusting your gut is still your best line of defense. The last thing you want to do is look back to your first meeting and wonder why you didn't trust your feelings.

To make sure you are not ignoring the signs of what you are observing and feeling, and to make sure your instincts are correct, go back to Chapter 1. Answer the questions in the three questionnaires, "Negative Emotion" Questionnaire, "How Does He Behave Toward You?" Questionnaire, and "How He Makes You Feel about Yourself" Questionnaire. If you answer Yes to any of the questions on any of the three questionnaires, you are in the presence of a man who is toxic to you.

If You See a Red Flag, Dig Deeper

Let's say your instincts are screaming that something is not right. What do you do? You ask questions—hard-hitting, get-to-the-bottom-line questions. You don't ask superficial "feel good" questions. If something a man says sounds farfetched or not right, don't ignore it. Instead, probe deeper. Ask more questions. Say things like:

- "Excuse me, I didn't quite catch what you said."
- "Can you explain further?"
- "What exactly do you mean by that?"
- "I'm not sure I follow you."

If he says something that *really* sounds unbelievable or makes you wonder, take the spotlight off yourself and put it on an imaginary third person by saying, "I know someone who would really question that" or "What do you say if someone tells you they find that hard to believe?" Then watch how he reacts to those questions. If he gets defensive, you've learned a lot. Something isn't right and you may want to limit your interaction with him. Don't let him get away with lies or made-up stories. If you do so, it will form the basis of a toxic business or social relationship. Never do business or socialize with someone whom you catch in a lie under any circumstances. After all, if he's comfortable lying, he's probably also comfortable doing a lot *worse* things too.

On the other hand, if you realize what is going on, maybe it is just enough for you to know and leave it and him at that—it depends on the circumstances.

Digging Deeper Still

Sometimes the questions in the previous section don't fully quell your doubts about a person. If that's the case, keep digging! Go deeper into your inquiry to get to the bottom of what is not sitting right with you. Don't worry about being politically correct or whether or not he'll think the question is weird. Remember, your well-being is at stake here! Speak up and say what's on your mind.

What you specifically ask depends on what you want to know. Your head may be filled with plenty of questions you have thought up on your own while interacting with him. If that's the case, go ahead and ask! You are free to ask whatever you want. But in case you need a little guidance, I compiled a list of questions that can serve as a guideline for you. They mostly pertain to interpersonal relationships.

Keep in mind that when you ask someone deeper questions, you may make them feel uncomfortable. Because you are probably not used to asking such probing questions, you may feel uncomfortable asking them. But don't let that stop you, because you would feel a lot more uncomfortable finding out that you have wasted a lot of time with someone who is not right for you. Therefore, these questions are definitely worth asking. Ask the ones that are relevant to you.

At first, you may feel a little awkward asking such direct questions. You can increase your comfort level by practicing these questions ahead of time. Read them aloud and then answer them yourself to better familiarize yourself with the words and phrases. You can also role-play with a friend and ask her the questions in order to help you feel more comfortable with them. Always remember to take a quick breath in through your mouth, hold it for a second, and then calmly ask your question on the airstream on which you simultaneously exhale.

If he is put off by any of your questions, that may be telling. He may have something to hide. Also pay attention to his body language. (You will learn more about how to read a person and what toxic body language and communication signs to look for in the next two chapters.)

PROBING QUESTIONS TO ASK

PERSONAL FEELINGS

1. How often do you lose your temper?
2. When was the last time you lied to someone?
3. What things mean a lot to you?
4. If you were super-angry, how would you like someone to react toward you?
5. What makes you feel guilty?
6. What's your biggest fear?
7. What's your biggest flaw?
8. What's the worst thing anyone has ever said about you?
9. What makes you cry?
10. What makes you so angry you could spit?
11. What was the worst thing you did when you were younger?
12. What are you ashamed of?
13. What is your biggest regret?
14. What makes you the angriest and how do you act when you are really mad?
15. How do you react when your feelings or ego are hurt?
16. What would you consider the greatest adventure you had or could have?
17. What things make you absolutely sick to your stomach?

RELATIONSHIPS

1. What are you really looking for in a woman ?
2. Who do you hate the most and why?
3. What happened in your marriage that broke you up?
4. What's your ideal view of marriage?
5. What would you do if you married someone and she gained a lot of weight?
6. What would you do if you married someone who went blind or couldn't walk?
7. Do you have ex-girlfriends with whom you are still friends and who you still see?
8. Under what circumstances would you cheat on someone?
9. What would you do if someone cheated on you?
10. What would you expect someone to do if you cheated on her?
11. What would you do if a woman's friends or relatives couldn't stand you?
12. What is your biggest turn-off and complaint about women you know?

CHILDREARING

1. How would you discipline a child if he were really bad?

FINANCIAL/WORK

1. How much money do you feel a person should have as a nest egg?
2. What were your last three jobs and how did they go?
3. Have you ever been fired? If so, why?
4. What would you do if someone swindled you out of your money?
5. If you could no longer do the work you do or were fired, what would you do?

FRIENDSHIPS

1. What is your biggest turn-off and complaint about men you know?
2. What qualities do you look for in a friend?

3. Who is your biggest enemy and why?
4. Who is your best friend and why?

FAMILY

1. What was your parents' relationship like with each other?
2. What was your relationship like with your dad, growing up and now?
3. What was your relationship like with your siblings early on and what is it like now?
4. What was your relationship like with your mom, growing up and now?

Of course, the key is to listen carefully to how he answers these questions. If you find yourself too quick to jump in or ask a follow-up question, try this technique: After you ask a question, breathe in, hold it, and gently bite the sides of your tongue. This will prevent you from asking another question. It will also make you conscious of the fact that you need to be listening to his answer and focusing on his body language.

Keep in mind that you don't have to ask every single one of these questions. Just pick the ones that are most important to you. Take your time when asking these questions and listen to his responses. Sometimes he will give an answer that will lead you to a question that is not on the list. In that case, go with the flow. Probe deeper in terms of what he revealed. Be careful not to bombard him with a slew of rapid-fire questions so that he feels as though you are interrogating him. He needs to feel that you are truly interested in his response as you digest his answer.

CHAPTER 9

Toxic Body Language Signals

How I Read Body Language from Photos and Videos

In my work as a body language expert and communication analyst, I find that pictures and videos really are worth a thousand words. I am often asked by media around the world to analyze the status of celebrity relationships based on photos and videos of celebrities and newsmakers. I even have a monthly column in *Cosmopolitan* magazine, "The Real Story," where I analyze what is really happening behind the headlines with newsmakers. I make this service available to the public as well via my website, *www.drlillianglass.com*, where anyone can upload their photos or videos of themselves or their loved ones and e-mail them to me to "read." After analyzing the body language, I tell them what I think is going on with them and their relationship. I also analyze body language of newsmakers in my Dr. Lillian Glass Body Language Blog, which describes what is really going on behind the headlines.

It is uncanny how accurate the information is when you know how to analyze photos and videos. I look for a number of things, such as:

- Facial expression and muscle tension in the face (if there is a lot of tension in the lower jaw, it usually spells anger)
- Whether smiles are genuine, as there are many different types of smiles that reveal different things
- In pictures of couples, how the individuals are leaning in relation to each other and what the spatial relationship is between them

- In pictures of couples, how their bodies, especially torsos and hips, are positioned in relation to each another, which communicates the status of the couple's sexual relationship
- What the hands are doing (e.g., a subconscious fistlike gesture with the hand definitely spells trouble)
- The positions of the legs and feet, which tell a lot about the level of security and self-confidence or whether members of a couple really like one another

My extensive experience in this area means that I can give you a wide range of accurate body language "tells." While there are a lot of books on the market on body language and how to read people, including my own book *I Know What You're Thinking: Using the Four Codes of Communication to Improve Your Life*, this book, *Toxic Men,* will tell you what the specific signals mean concerning toxicity in your relationships.

Facial and body language analysis is a must to master because it can give you the heads-up that something is wrong in your relationship, marriage, or business dealings. First, let's learn to look at toxic facial expressions and body language and find out what messages are really being conveyed.

Reading a Man's Face

To accurately tell how a man really feels about you, it is essential to know how to read his facial expressions. That is why whenever you speak to a man, you must always look at his face to pick up subtle cues. That is why it is so important to not go to the movies or take a car drive or engage in other activities where you can't see a man's face when you go on a first date with him. Instead, go to a restaurant or coffee shop, where you can sit directly across from him and look right at his face as you engage in conversation.

HOW TO LOOK AT HIS FACE

When looking at a man, don't just stare at his eyes—look at his entire face so that you can pick up all the important facial cues he gives off with his forehead, eyes, nose, cheeks, lips, and chin. It will also give you an opportunity to look for any skin changes, such as whether he is turning red with anger or pale with fear.

First, spend a second looking at his forehead, then move down to look at his eyes and brows for a second, his nose for a second, and then his cheeks for a second. Then move to his mouth, lips, and chin. Finally, look at his entire face for two seconds. Keep repeating this exercise as you look at each part of his face for a second and then focus on the bigger picture—his entire face for two seconds. You need to be doing this throughout your entire conversation with him. At first it may seem awkward, but the more you practice doing it, the more comfortable you will feel communicating with this man. You will be surprised at the facial cues you will pick up that tell you everything you need to know. Note that this scrutiny will not look peculiar to the man because the eye movements you will use are so subtle that he won't notice.

SUDDEN FACIAL CHANGES

It's also important to look for anything that causes a change in his facial expression. Since you'll be watching his face constantly, it's relatively easy to notice these changes. While his face may be saying one thing one moment, you may suddenly see a flash of emotion "leaking out" on his face that tells you what he *really* thinks of you or a situation. For instance, you may see a cool, calm, and collected expression and then all of a sudden you may see him quickly raise his upper lip and wrinkle his nose while spreading out his lower lip so you see his bottom teeth, indicating disgust at what you said or did.

WHAT'S A GENUINE SMILE?

Even if a man seems to be smiling at you, he may not really be happy to see you. If his lips are together and he looks as if he is smiling, he is only truly happy if his eyes are also crinkled, his cheekbones are raised, and you see his teeth while his lips are parted. Only that constitutes a genuine smile.

If you see his teeth and he looks directly into your eyes, has a slightly protruding lower lip while flaring his nostrils, and his breathing is visible to you, you can bet he's not only into you, he may even be turned on or in love with you.

THE IMPORTANCE OF EYEBROWS

When you first greet a man and his eyebrows aren't raised, chances are that he is not thrilled to see you. When a man sees someone he likes, he does an "eyebrow flash," where he raises his eyebrows and opens his eyes wide. So if his eyebrows are not flashing when he sees you, it is not a good sign. If you are on a blind date and you don't see this gesture as soon as he meets you, rest assured you are off to a very bad start.

HEAD MOVEMENTS

If you see him jerk his head back after you have told him something, he may literally be taken aback by what you just said to him. If you see that he suddenly raises his chin and juts his jaw out, it may indicate that he is upset or angry at something you did or said.

Keep the Conversation in Mind

It's important to keep all of the movements and emotions we'll discuss in this chapter in proper perspective. Just seeing a shoulder shrug may indicate he has an itch. The same holds true if he scratches his nose. A scratch may just be a scratch. But if you ask him if he was with Gina last night and he shrugs and scratches, then it is a different matter. If he does this after saying no, he's probably lying to you about where he spent the night.

So, when you see an expression or movement that seems to indicate a negative emotion or a lack of interest in you, be sure you consider exactly what caused his reaction.

List of Facial Expressions that Project Negative Emotions

Following is a rundown of what a man's face shows when he feels a certain way. It is in your best interest to become very familiar with this list as a point of reference. You don't have to memorize it verbatim, but you should know what to look for with regard to each specific emotion.

- **Sadness:** Eyebrows are lowered. Forehead is wrinkled. Lower lip is depressed. Lack of eye contact. Looks down a lot. Lack of visual focus. Often blank and unanimated expression. Tight-lipped smile not showing teeth and often downward slope of lips.
- **Anger:** Eyebrows are lowered. Stare is hard. Both lips are raised. Mouth is open. Lower jaw protrudes. Chin juts forward. Lower teeth are bared. Face color is often red or flushed. Wide nasal flare on both nostrils.
- **Fear:** Eyebrows are raised. Upper eyelids are raised. Lips are stretched (contorted). Mouth is open. Pale-colored or ashen-colored face. Hand is on one cheek. Sweating on temples or upper lip.
- **Disgust:** Upper lip is raised. Nose is wrinkled. Mouth is open. Chin is raised.
- **Doubt:** Head is lowered or turned and cocked to one side. Eyes squint. Strokes chin. Pinches bridge of nose. Rubs eyes.
- **Boredom:** Vacant stare. Blank facial expressions. Jaw shifted to one side. Nose slightly flared. Lips down and open. No eye or facial contact with the other person. Looks at others in the room instead of at you. Repetitive lip-biting or lip-smacking. Hands on both cheeks.

Reading a Man's Body

Just as it is important to look at a man's face for clues, you should pay close attention to what he doing with his body. You must be aware of signals he is giving off with his posture and body movements, how much space he is taking up, how close to you or far away from you he is, and what he is doing with his hands and feet. Here are some common body movements that reveal a man's emotions:

- **Shoulder shrug:** If a man says that he doesn't know anything about geophysics or how to program his DVR and shrugs his shoulders, he may very well be telling the truth. But if he tells you something that may not be true (about a former relationship or other sensitive topic), you may also suddenly see him shrug his shoulders. Depending on what you are discussing, if a man suddenly shrugs his shoulders when he is telling you that he didn't do something, he may be lying to you.
- **Foot movements:** If you see him pointing his feet in the opposite direction of you, he may literally want to get away from you and leave. He definitely does not like being around you.
- **Rocking motion:** If he's rocking back and forth when he's talking to you, he's uncomfortable around you and wants to get away as soon as possible.
- **Covering his chest:** If he covers his chest by placing one of his arms on his opposite shoulder, he may be indicating he is closing off to you or he may even be intimidated by you. If he's fiddling with his hands, this may also reveal that he is feeling intimidated.

List of Body Language Signals That Project Negative Emotions

This list shows you how a man's body tells you what he's feeling. Again, you don't need to memorize the list, but be sure you remember enough to know how each emotion will show itself.

- **Sadness:** Lethargic. Slow body movement. Slumped shoulders. Head often bowed. Limited gestures. Jerky movements. Visible sighing with chest heaving.
- **Anger:** Closed body posture. Clenched or cupped hands in a fistlike position, kicking movements with legs. Leaning forward. Invading another's body space.

- **Fear:** Rubbing vulnerable areas of body, such as the throat. Observable pulse on neck. Sweating on body. Tension in shoulders. Holding breath. Elbows drawn to the sides. Legs tightly crossed over one another. One leg wrapped around the other. Fidgeting.
- **Disgust:** Steps back. Jerks head back. Tension in shoulders and extremities.
- **Doubt:** Hiding hands in pockets may show ambivalence. Scratching head. Hand on neck. Hand on cheek. Eye rubbing.
- **Boredom:** Fidgeting with hands. Doing other activities with hands (doodling, writing, fixing or fiddling with a mechanical device or a cell phone). Looking at cell phone or checking watch often. Repeated hand actions such as drumming or tapping fingers on table. Swinging legs. Tapping toes. Shaking feet. The more bored, the more quickly they tap, drum, swing, or shake their extremities. Posture is slouched with rounded shoulders. Head is down. Leaning away from you or leaning on a table, chair, wall, or object. Many deep breaths and yawning.

A Dozen Signals That Say "I Am Not into You"

The face and body language already discussed can give you signs that he may not be into you, or that he may be toxic to you. But the following signals are definite tells that he's not interested in you. Do not overlook them. Paying close attention to these specific signs will save you a lot of embarrassment, anguish, and wasted time with someone who has no interest in you.

1. Leans his body away from you when sitting or standing
2. Rocks back and forth or shakes a foot or leg or taps a finger
3. Backs away from you when you attempt to move closer
4. Crosses his arms over his torso with hands on opposite shoulders
5. Puts his feet in the opposite direction to yours
6. Keeps his palms down when he speaks to you and gestures toward his body

7. Maintains overall tension or muscle stiffness in his body
8. Holds on to himself or to an arm or his hands as if he is bracing himself
9. Steeples his hands in front of his mouth, indicating judgment of you, or puts a hand or finger over his mouth indicating he doesn't want to talk to you
10. Constantly breaks eye contact to look at someone or something else
11. Doesn't look at you full face, but rather at an angle from the side
12. Shows a tight-lipped smile (not showing teeth) or won't smile at all
13. Eyes not smiling and cheeks not raised

When a man is not into you, don't ignore the signs. Even though it is hurtful to your ego, get out of denial. See what is, not what isn't. He may not be into you for a number of reasons, so don't bother trying to guess or wait to find out why. He may not be physically attracted to you, or perhaps he's intimidated by you. Don't dwell on the fact that he doesn't appear interested—be proud of yourself for deciphering his body language and facial expressions before you wasted further time with him.

A Dozen Signals That Say "I'm Not Being Honest"

Displaying one or two of these signals doesn't necessarily mean that he's lying. However, the more signals you see, the greater the chance he isn't telling you the truth.

1. Shoulder shrug
2. Lip-licking due to dry mouth; lip-pursing, lip-biting
3. Gulping or visible hard swallowing
4. Not moving hands; hands stationary on lap
5. Limited eye contact; breaks eye contact a lot or blinks excessively
6. Staring and little facial animation; masklike expression
7. Fidgeting
8. Shoulders hunched and head bowed is indicating shame or embarrassment

9. Foot shuffling and movement
10. Hand on neck
11. Nose, ear, head, or body scratching
12. Sweating, especially on forehead and upper lip

Once again, it is essential to consider the context when interpreting these signals of deception. Think about the topic of conversation and the question you just asked.

If You See Warning Signs, Move On

If you see any of the facial or body language signs given in this chapter that aren't attributable to harmless or benign causes, cut your interaction short and be on your way. If you see any in your relationship, there is major trouble brewing. (Your relationship may require heavy doses of communication therapy and counseling sessions.)

If you see the signs in your professional or business relationships, you may want to ask some probing questions. The questions you ask depend on what you specifically want to know in terms of your particular business enterprise or your career. Therefore, I can't provide you with a specific list of questions as I did when discussing romantic relationship questions. But know that you must always be direct. Get to the point and don't beat around the bush or couch your questions in a tentative manner. Use a rich tone when you speak so that you sound more confident. You can do this by pushing out your abdominal muscles as you speak. In order to make sure that your voice doesn't waver and that you sound more confident and in control, remember to breathe in, hold your breath for a second, and then ask your question on your exhaled breath. Listen carefully to the entire answer. You may also ask the same question in different ways in order to make sure that there is consistency in his answer and that he is not lying to you. If you are unsatisfied with the answer, you may want to do business elsewhere.

CHAPTER 10

Listening to WHAT He Says and HOW He Says It

Toxic Voice Patterns

The ancient Greek philosopher Galen was correct when he said that it is the "voice that mirrors the soul." The voice is a barometer for what is going on inside of a person. It tells you not only how a man feels about himself, but also how he feels about you. After spending the past two decades researching the subject and helping people enhance their vocal tones, I have come to observe firsthand how the voice mirrors one's personality or emotional state. You can tell so much just by listening to the tone of a voice and how things are said.

Knowing how to "read" a man's vocal tone can give you a great deal of insight into both his psyche and his personality. There are a lot of things a Toxic Man conveys without using words, facial expressions, or body language. His toxic message can be conveyed by the rate, volume, and quality of his voice. In this chapter, you will see what toxic messages or emotional tells can be conveyed via vocal behaviors.

Toxic Vocal Tells

A man's voice is a barometer that not only will tell you how he is feeling but also will give you a great deal of insight into his personality and what he is really thinking. That is why it is essential to listen not just to what a man says but to how he says it as well.

CAUTION: "I'M NOT SURE HOW I FEEL ABOUT YOU OR WHETHER I LIKE YOU"

Men who tend to be unsure or indecisive about you do a number of things that are reflected in their voices. If he isn't sure how he feels about you or about something you have done, you will often hear his vocal pitch get higher, especially at the end of sentences. Through his voice, he is leaking out doubt or ambivalence toward you.

ANGER: "I'M MEAN, ANGRY, HOSTILE, AND COMPETITIVE AND I DON'T LIKE YOU"

Men who are angry and hostile not only speak at a louder volume but they will always have a hard glottal attack, meaning they attack with their words in a harsh, staccato manner using the back of their throat muscles. Men who attack with their tones—often choppy bursts of staccato and loudness—are usually angry, aggressive, and competitive types. Such a man's voice gives you little shocks of hostility—machine-gun-like blasts of anger spewing forth throughout his conversation. These inappropriate sudden bursts of tone makes him sound as though he has a belligerent or defensive attitude, and is looking for a fight or an argument.

Angry speakers also speak at a rapid clip. The speed of their speech is often indicative of how angry they feel at the time. When a man is angry at you for achieving more than him, you will often hear him speak very quickly. He will speak fast as he bombards you with question after question about various issues in an attempt to perhaps trip you up and then show you that you have made a mistake. He does this to show oneupmanship so that he can make himself feel less insecure around you.

And yet another way a man may show anger in his voice is by speaking in a monotone, especially when the occasion calls for an animated tone. It is anger that is held back in a passive-aggressive way.

And lastly, when you see someone who doesn't open his jaws when he speaks and has a nasal tone, so that the sound seems to be coming from his nose and not his throat, rest assured that he is an angry man. As the late and great acting coach Nina Foch used to say, "A lock-jawed man is an angry man."

INSECURITY: "I'M INSECURE, ESPECIALLY ABOUT MY MANLINESS"

Any man who deepens his voice by forcing it an octave lower usually feels insecure about himself. He overcompensates with this vocal tone to try to make people perceive him as being more powerful than he is. Insecure men also have a tendency to talk louder in order to gain more attention.

I should also point out that sometimes when a man speaks in an excessively loud voice, he may be suffering from a hearing loss. In order to make sure, simply ask the man politely if he has a hearing loss or if anything is interfering with his hearing. A client of mine did this and discovered that the man she was dating had been in a rock band when he was younger, and as a result suffered significant hearing loss.

EGOCENTRICITY: "I DESPERATELY NEED TO BE THE CENTER OF ATTENTION"

Men who speak in a very loud or very deep voice are screaming that they need others to notice them. They speak like this all the time, even when it's not appropriate.

CONDESCENSION: "I'M BETTER THAN YOU"

When a man speaks to you in overarticulated, choppy, and deliberate tones, it often indicates that he is being condescending and is very inflexible. If he is very precise, and there is little, if any, room for you to interject, it shows that he is pompous and arrogant and thinks he knows everything. You may feel as though you are being spoken down to, or as if he is speaking to a child, which, since you are an adult, is very disrespectful.

EVIL INTENTIONS: "I'M GOING TO MANIPULATE YOU"

When a man speaks to you in overinflected tones, where he sounds like the stereotype of a hyped-up salesman with a lot of "razzle dazzle" trying to sell you a bill of goods, chances are that he is doing just that. He is trying to suck you in. He is trying way too hard to convince you to believe his point of view. It can be very alluring, but when a man uses this overamped, high-drama vocal inflection, be cautious. More than likely, he is trying to sell you on something for *his* benefit.

NARCISSISM: "IT'S ABOUT ME, NOT YOU"

When a man speaks rapidly, he isn't thinking about you getting the message. He is thinking about himself. It is very common to hear these men spew out information as they speak *at* you, not *with* you. This is often the case with self-oriented or perhaps narcissistic men. Often these selfish "It's all about me" type of men will speak in louder vocal tones as well.

APATHY: "I REALLY DON'T CARE AND I'M NOT REALLY HAPPY FOR YOU"

When something good happens to you and you hear a man's monotonous drone saying the words "That's great. I'm really happy for you," or "That's exciting," know that he does not think it's great, nor is he happy or excited for you. If he meant those things, you would definitely hear more excitement in his voice. There would be some inflection to convey the emotion behind what he said to you.

A lot of people who suffer from depression speak in this type of lifeless monotone voice, so you should be aware of that possibility as well. But if the man isn't suffering from depression or isn't sad about something in particular, he should not sound monotonous. He may also be the type of man who withholds his emotions. This trait can prove to be frustrating over time, especially if you are engaged in an interpersonal relationship with him.

PASSIVE-AGGRESSION: "CAN YOU PLEASE SPEAK UP?"

Earlier, you read about a trick of the Sneaky Passive-Aggressor type in which the volume of his voice dies off at the end of sentences in order to get people to ask him to repeat things. He secretly enjoys these little power trips. When you meet a man who consciously makes his voice inaudible at the end of sentences, suspect that he may be passive-aggressive and highly manipulative.

POWER: "I NEED TO CONTROL YOU"

When a man talks *at* you and goes on and on and on and ignores you, he is clearly exhibiting characteristics of a controlling man. He may speak super-slowly, so you feel as though you could fly from Los Angeles to New York City by the time he finishes a sentence. It is his way of gaining vocal control over you by literally forcing you to listen to him until he finishes what he has to say. Heaven forbid you should try to interrupt him. He will either admonish you for it, by telling you that he is not finished speaking, or he will completely ignore you.

DISHONESTY: "I'M LYING"

When a man lies, several things may occur. His voice may get shaky, causing a little tremor in his tone. You may also hear "pitch breaks" in his voice, where the pitch suddenly changes. (This is due to tension that arises in the throat muscles when someone is not telling the truth.) You may also hear a lot of throat-clearing and throat noises, mainly because the mouth gets drier when a person is lying. He may also tend to speed up his speech when nervous. That's because he wants to hurry up and quickly get out all the untruthful information.

Toxic Speech Patterns

Just as a man's voice speaks volumes, so do the actual words he says. That is why it is essential for you to listen carefully to every word a man says. To do that, you need to listen more than you speak, according to my dear friend Dr. Paul Cantalupo. He used to say that this is why we have two ears and one mouth—so we can listen twice as much as we speak. He also used to say that if you let someone talk long enough, he will reveal everything about himself.

When you listen carefully to what a man says, he will leak out a lot of information about himself, especially in terms of how he relates to others.

Does he constantly speak ill of others? Does he seem to get involved in deals where he gets the best of others, or involved in deals where others get the best of him? When he speaks of women in his past, is he vengeful or does the woman always seem like the victim? Is he often in some conflict with someone?

This is very important information for you to know, whether you work with a man, are employed by him, are his employer, are dating him, are thinking of marrying him, or are already married to him. It is essential to know what a man really means by what he says. In the past, you may have ignored many things he said that could have communicated toxicity. The information you will read now will change the way you listen to a man forever.

IF HE GIVES YOU WAY TOO MUCH INFORMATION

If you have just met a man and he tells you a ton of information about *everything*—his kid's bed-wetting problem, his horrible ex-wife, or his failed business relationships—he may want your sympathy, especially if he "reads" that you are a nurturing type. It may be his way of trying to bond with you too quickly. But as you know, relationships take time and effort to develop, so his intense bonding attempt may be a way of trying to quickly gain your confidence so he can manipulate you.

It also shows that he has very little, if any, in the way of personal boundaries. It's one thing to hear about these things if you have known the man a while, but if he blurts out this information soon after you first meet him, it is a big red flag. If he shares the most intimate details about his ex-wife's bedroom habits or shares information that others no doubt told him in confidence, it also means that anything you share with him may eventually become public knowledge. So be aware that this is a man with poor judgment who has difficulties withholding information.

If he gossips about others and tells tales out of school, he has little or no loyalty and you may be gossiped about as well. Be careful about what you tell him. A man with no loyalty or boundaries may very well become your worst enemy one day.

One more thing: if a man goes on and on about his illness and talks to you about how sick he is, he either wants your sympathy or he wants to turn you off. It may be the bait he throws out to see how you will react. If you say "poor thing" and indulge him, you may end up being his next nurse or caretaker. Men usually want to put their best foot forward, even if they aren't quite feeling up to par. So if he tells you about all his illnesses and surgeries in detail and puts his worst foot forward, he may be purposely trying to turn you off. If it's your first date and he isn't attracted to you, he may set you up by saying he isn't feeling well but came on the date anyway. This way, he can bow out quickly.

IF HE'S OVERLY SARCASTIC

Men who use a lot of sarcasm say mean things like, "Here, have another doughnut, you wear it well—I'm just kidding," are *not* just kidding. In this case, he actually thinks you are fat and if you eat another doughnut it will make you look even fatter. These "kidders" are showing you that they aren't happy about you or something you did or didn't do, are jealous of you, or harbor some inner hostility toward you. A man who makes jokes at your expense is a man who has some resentment toward you.

Also, note that if you tell a man something serious, such as that you are sick or you have a serious problem, and he laughs at you, belittles you, or minimizes the situation, that is a huge red flag. It speaks to his lack of compassion and sensitivity toward you and may also be an indication of sadistic behavior, where he actually enjoys your bad predicament.

IF HE PUTS YOU DOWN

If a man puts you down or says something like "You have a college degree and don't know that?" or "You live here in town and don't know about this place?" it means that he feels so insecure about himself that he has to put you down and belittle you in order to make himself feel better. If he contradicts practically everything you say, he is especially insecure. The more he contradicts and shows how much he can "one-up" you, the more insecure he is. If he begins to vigorously debate you, he has something he is trying to prove to you. It may be on a topic that is not debatable or ridiculous, such as why you should have a car with four doors rather than two doors, why chocolate is better than vanilla, why big dogs are better to have than small dogs, or why dogs are better than cats. If a man constantly brags about himself and tells you about all of his accomplishments and how great he is, this is also a signal of insecurity and of having something to prove.

Another sign of insecurity is if the man talks at you, and in essence is lecturing you. A man who is insecure will also bombard you with a series of questions and make cutting remarks to your answers. Sometimes an insecure man will make a rude remark or make a shocking comment just to get your attention. He may enjoy watching you become unglued when he criticizes your appearance or something you are wearing. The entire charade is nothing more than a power trip on his part. To compensate for his insecurity, he does as much as he can to be in charge.

There is one more tactic that a man will use if he is insecure and intimidated by a woman: he'll cut himself down. He may try to be self-effacing, in the hopes that you will build him up. He may tear himself down or negate or minimize himself, saying that he's really not that great or not that smart, in the hope that you will disagree with him and say something positive to build up his fragile ego.

IF HE TALKS CONSTANTLY ABOUT HIMSELF

Any man who constantly talks about himself doesn't respect you. He is usually selfish and self-centered. If he asks very few, or no, questions of you, or if he offers very little feedback about what you uttered, you may as well keep quiet and not waste your breath because he won't hear you anyway. He is too consumed with himself to care about what anyone else says or thinks.

Another clue to a man's selfishness is if he flits from topic to topic, just discussing what he wants to discuss. If you bring up a topic and he changes it, this is not a good sign. Neither is a man who interrupts you excessively. These tactics are power plays: he is trying to tell you that he is in charge and that you are not that important.

HOW TO TELL IF HE'S LYING TO YOU

There are many indications men will give that they are lying to you. Here are some common signs:

- Whenever you hear him repeat words or phrases or answer a question with a question, he is usually not telling you the truth.
- "Filler" words and phrases such as "um," "like, um," "er," "eh," or "you know" also mean that he may not be telling you the truth.
- Another signal that he is lying is if he gives you way to much information. Let's say you asked him casually where he was last night. If he gives you a detailed version of where he was and diverts the story by going off on different tangents, chances are he is not telling the truth. When he says he went to the bar and then he had a flat tire and tells you about how Joe helped him (and how Joe went to school with him and has a baby on the way and Joe's wife is really a mean person), know that he may have been at the bar with a Jo all night, but it may have been Jo Anne. Going off on tangents like that and answering a simple question in too much detail are big red flags. People give more information than they need to when they lie as a means of compensating. They are trying too hard to convince you that they are telling the truth so they give you even more information than is necessary or relevant.
- Defensiveness is also a huge tell when a man is not being forthright. If he tries to turn the tables on you or makes irrelevant accusations toward you, chances are he has something to hide.
- If a man doesn't openly share information with you, or you feel as if you are pulling his teeth when talking to him, he may have something to hide. The same is true if he bombards you with question after question. He may be trying to get something out of you, such as valuable information he needs. By having more

information about you than you have about him, he can more easily control where the conversation will go. For example, if a married man is trying to hit on you, he will often ask a lot more questions than he answers.

- Finally, listen for inconsistencies. If you think the story sounds too good to be true or too far-fetched to be true, you are probably right. If you want to verify whether he is lying, remind him sometime later that day or the next week about the story (lie) he told you. Ask him to tell it again because you were so interested. Most likely, he will oblige. Then listen for changes and information that doesn't match his previous story (lie).

When Not to Get Offended By a Man's Communication

Although these toxic communication methods are annoying to a lot of women, some of the things men say and do in the workplace and in their personal lives should not be taken as a slight or as an insult. There is no malice or anything toxic behind these behaviors.

For example, because of the way they have been raised and conditioned, men tend to use more command terms, like "Get me this" or "Go here" or "Give me that." If you watch little boys at play, you'll see that they use very few terms of politeness and endearment. When you watch little girls at play, however, it is the exact opposite—they say, "Please get me this" or they ask, "Would you go here?" Unfortunately, these communication tendencies carry over into adulthood. It makes for a lot of misunderstanding and miscommunication between the sexes. So if you hear a command without a question or a "please" from a man, don't get too rattled—it's just a guy thing.

The same holds true for interruptions. Men have a tendency to interrupt more than women. Unless it's excessive, it's normal male communication behavior and nothing to be concerned about.

Another instance of men and women tending to act differently is how they speak when they're nervous or uncomfortable in a new situation.

When women break the ice and bond, they usually do it with compliments. But men do it with jokes. Unless the jokes are about you, consider it a male communication method and don't be concerned.

If He Says He's a Jerk or a Bad Boy, He Probably Is!

This piece of advice may seem unnecessary to give, but in my experience, women often overlook it: If a man tells you that he's a jerk, or that he's not that smart, or that he's a loser, believe him! Don't disagree with him or try to convince him how great he is. Too many women do this because they don't want to hurt the man's feelings or they want to "make nice" and placate the man. They want the man to think that they like him and that, unlike others, they would never think anything negative about him. It is their attempt to be liked by letting the man know that they like him. If you find yourself doing this, stop. You don't need to be overly nice or be so polite in order to be perceived as being likeable. Instead, open your ears to hearing the truth. Stop convincing yourself that he is more than he said he is and instead listen to valuable information a man reveals about himself from his own lips. If a man says something negative about himself or tells you he is a jerk, what you need to say is "Thank you for letting me know," "I'll keep that in mind," or "I'm glad you shared that with me. I won't forget it."

When they look back at their toxic relationship with the man who called himself a jerk or a bad boy, many women could have saved themselves a lot of time and energy if they had believed the negative information they heard. They would never have been emotionally invested with the self-described jerk or bad boy in the first place.

Listen to a man's history, especially for the following issues:

- Listen for clues that let you know if he is in debt.
- Does he seem to be is in trouble with the law or have a lot of legal issues pending?
- Listen to information he gives about his kids. Are they troubled?

- Listen to what he says about his ex. Does he despise her? Is he filled with hate or are they best friends to the point where he is still dependent on her?

This information will allow you to think with your head and not only with your heart. Your head and your heart must work together in choosing the right man, so pay close attention to every word that comes out of his mouth.

CHAPTER 11

Culture Clash Warning!

Toxic Versus Different

People from different cultures may not see their own behavior as toxic; it's just what their culture or religion believes is right or good or the best way to do things. But you may see it as toxic if the two of you are not on the same page or you cannot see things from one another's point of view. If you think his behavior is toxic and he doesn't (because of his cultural or religious beliefs), you probably aren't a good fit for a romantic relationship. If you two can meet in the middle, then you have a very good chance at a successful relationship.

The Good News about Globalization

With the ease of world travel and the wide exposure to people from different cultures, the world has become a much smaller place, with fewer and fewer physical boundaries. Having traveled around the world and met people from various cultures through my lectures abroad, I have discovered that we are more alike than we are different. We feel the same pain when we are sick or injured, and feel the same grief when we lose someone we love. We all crave enough food in our bellies so that we never go hungry. We all desire a comfortable shelter to protect us from nature's harsh elements. We all want to feel safe, protected, loved, and respected.

As travelers from Western cultures interact with more and more people from different cultures and hear them describe their wants and desires, it's clear that famed psychologist Abraham Maslow's Hierarchy of Needs is quite accurate. Developed in 1943, the Hierarchy of Needs is: physical needs (air, food, sleep), security needs (clothing, safety), social needs (friendship, romance, family), the need for esteem (social recognition), and the need for self-actualization (self-awareness, personal growth). Whether you are a Maasai in Kenya, an Aborigine in Australia, a New York businessman, or a Beverly Hills matron, you all share the exact same emotions, make the same facial expressions, and even make the same tones as one another when you express those emotions. I have witnessed this up close during my travels, concurring with the landmark studies on human emotion by Dr. Paul Ekman at the University of California, San Francisco.

Because of globalization, we seem to have less fear and more understanding of others who may look and sound different than ourselves than in any other time in history. This leads us to more openly embrace and accept those who cultural opposites.

When Cultural Opposites Work Out

If you end up in a relationship with a man from a culture that is different from yours, you may experience traditions that you may not like, don't want to participate in, find offensive, or that are contrary to who you are or what you believe in. On the other hand, one of the great benefits of being involved with a man who has a different religion or culture is that the experience may enhance your perspective on various issues.

While any relationship takes a lot of work and understanding, cross-cultural relationships require much more effort from both sides. That's not to say that you shouldn't get involved with someone who is extremely different from you culturally; just know that there is a lot to consider, depending on the culture and how steeped he is in that culture.

Before you make a serious commitment, you both need to lay out on the table all issues for potential conflict.

Consider these topics:

- You need to know what your man expects from you after marriage. Are you to stay at home and raise the kids or is he okay with your being a working mom?
- How about the day-to-day chores? Does he plan to pitch in, cook, and clean, or does he see that as strictly your domain?
- How about kids? How many does he want and what is his view on discipline?
- Does he eventually plan to return to his native country to live and to take his family there?
- Does he plan to have his parents live with you? If he is, are you expected to take care of them?
- Will you be required to participate in cultural rituals and be expected know how to perform them?
- Will you be required to learn his native language?

You must know these things in order to determine whether you are on the same page and whether your relationship has a future.

My Canadian friend Olivia cringed when she initially walked barefoot behind Raj, her Indian-born husband. Now she thinks nothing of walking barefoot behind him whenever they leave Canada and visit his family in Delhi. It is part of her life, as is learning to cook Indian food and observing all Hindu holidays and customs. In fact, she feels healthier than ever before now that she is a vegetarian. She lives in the same house with his parents, whom she adores. She was never particularly close to her own parents, who both worked and with whom she never spent time. Now she spends all her time with her husband's parents and loves it. She loves their attention and their warmth. She loves experiencing the closeness that she never had with her own parents. They appreciate her learning Hindi, and she loves making the parents of her husband happy. For her an added bonus is the extended family of aunts and uncles and cousins and brothers-in-law and sisters-in-law. She loves attending the celebrations, which seem to take place all the time because there are so many family members. She feels reborn in her new culture.

When Cultural Opposites Don't Work Out

Unfortunately, cross-cultural relationships also face a number of difficult obstacles, some of which may be too significant to overcome. Here are some of the most common challenges you may face if you're in this type of relationship.

MISCOMMUNICATION

The biggest problem in intercultural relationships is communication. Even though the two of you may speak the same language, miscommunications and misunderstandings can still occur because of the subtle nuances of languages. Usually you have to be raised in a culture or with a language to fully appreciate underlying humor or the tone in which something is said or meant. If you don't understand these fine elements, it is easy to misinterpret and misread, causing friction and irreparable damage.

Sometimes an accent or dialect can get in the way of meaning and understanding. When Rebecca first began dating her Chinese boyfriend, his Cantonese accent was very strong. She finally realized that his loud tones didn't mean he was angry or yelling at her, but were just a part of the way he spoke. His intonation was pleasing to the Chinese ear, but jarring to her American ear.

She told me about a time she thought about breaking up with him after he told her he brought her some locusts to eat. She firmly told him that she did not eat insects and locusts were disgusting. He insisted "locusts" were delicious and sweet. They went back and forth on this matter until he wrote the word "lotus" on a piece of paper. She laughed. He was gifting her with delicious lotus fruit, not locusts or grasshoppers.

Even if you and your partner both speak English, he may insist that you learn his native language in order to communicate with the rest of his family. If it's not something you are willing to do or you don't think you can do it, say that right away. You can't just sweep it under the rug and hope it goes away. It will undoubtedly come up again during the course of your relationship. Likewise, you can ask your partner to try to learn *your* language. There must be a mutual give-and-take relationship, where both are working for common good and understanding in the relationship. In order for the relationship to work, you have to both be willing to teach one another and to openly learn from one another. You can each take formal classes in the other's language, and help each other with your respective homework. This will increase your closeness, too.

UNSPOKEN EXPECTATIONS

I cannot stress enough the importance of communicating exactly what your expectations are before you marry someone from a different culture. I also cannot stress enough the importance of looking at a man's toxic behavior before marriage, as that is often how he will act during the marriage. It is also important to consider the potential dark side of any intercultural relationship and become informed regarding the laws of your prospective spouse's country. Will they automatically support his rights over yours in a marital or parental conflict?

Cheryl was raised in the heartland of the United States—Peoria, Illinois. She had a simple upbringing, going to public school, attending church on Sundays, and playing with friends much like her—white, middle class, with a father who worked at Caterpillar and a mother who stayed at home with the kids. It wasn't until she went away to college that she met people who were different from her, such as dark and swarthy Reza from Iran, a classmate on a student visa. She fell in love with Reza at first sight.

Signs of trouble began to brew when she met Reza's mother, a dominant, overly emotional woman who took an immediate dislike to Cheryl. She wanted her only son to marry a Persian woman and made this perfectly clear. But Reza had other ideas in mind—namely, becoming a U.S. citizen. Shortly after his mother returned to Iran, he began to be short-tempered, irritable, and controlling with Cheryl. He even mentioned to Cheryl that he wanted them to live in Iran after they married, had a family, and he earned a lot of money in the United States. She ignored it and just shrugged it off to him missing his mother.

Married life wasn't great for Cheryl, as she and Reza constantly fought. They had a roller-coaster relationship. Most fights were over his jealously, possessiveness, and attempts to control her. He tried to tell her when she could see her parents, with which friends she could associate, how much money she could spend (even though she was the breadwinner), and even what clothes she could wear when she ventured out of the house. His false accusations regarding her flirting with male coworkers were a source of contention as well. Even though she regularly found herself wanting to leave him, he would always sweet-talk and charm her into staying.

He convinced her that having a baby would be the answer to their problems and ease the tension between them. Willing to give anything a try in order to make the marriage work, Cheryl agreed. Yet their gorgeous little girl Layla's presence only made tensions greater because Reza took control over Layla, too. He alone decided when she would eat, sleep, and even be toilet-trained—at nine months of age. Cheryl put her foot down. Reza ignored her pleas and even spanked Layla when she soiled her diaper. Cheryl picked up the phone to call social services. Reza insisted she put down the phone and promised her he would refrain from any further attempts to toilet train or discipline Layla. Additionally, he turned up his charm meter full blast.

Early one Saturday morning Reza told Cheryl he had a birthday surprise for her. He took her to a fancy day spa in the city, where he booked her for a complete day of beauty. He told her that he would baby-sit Layla all day and that he and the baby would come and pick Cheryl up around 5 P.M. Cheryl was thrilled. But at 5 P.M., there was no Reza and no Layla to meet her. She repeatedly called her home and his cell phone, but there was no answer. She waited until 7 P.M., when the spa closed. Worried, she called one of the few girlfriends she still had left to pick her up.

On the way home, Cheryl made frantic calls to the police, and to hospitals in the area looking for her husband and little girl. When she arrived home, she found all of Layla's clothing and toys gone. There was a note in Layla's crib that read, "We went home to Iran. Don't ever expect to see me or your daughter again!" To say Cheryl was devastated is an understatement. She tried everything, including going to Iran to get her daughter. There was no one to help her. There was nothing the U.S. government could do, as laws in Iran favored her husband and there were no pertinent global treaties that applied.

UNREALISTIC EXPECTATIONS

Not only may the cultural hurdles be too difficult for you to leap, but your expectations may not be in sync with his. That is why it is essential for you both to communicate your expectations at the beginning of the relationship. Learn about his culture and ask point-blank if he eventually wants to live back in his native country. Learn about his politics and his view of the world. Ask what he expects from a wife and a marriage. Ask about his views on disciplining children and finances. Find out how he feels about a working woman. Really listen to what he says, not what you *want* him to say. Don't try to convert him to your way of thinking. In the long run, you may be unable or unwilling to adapt and vice versa.

DOMESTIC VIOLENCE ACROSS THE GLOBE

Many non-Western societies around the world have certain expectations for men and for women. There are specific roles and certain behaviors to which women must adhere. If women deviate from particular cultural norms, the consequences can range from unpleasant treatment to death. According to the World Health Organization, in places where the rate of domestic violence is high around the globe, it's due in large part to:

1. The unequal balance of power between couples
2. The "blame the victim" mentality
3. The shame that a woman's behavior would bring to the family
4. The indifference of state officials in many of these cultures to investigate and prosecute instances of domestic violence

Unfortunately, what most Americans consider normal behavior, such as disagreeing with your husband or questioning what he is doing, may result in other countries in legal beatings and physical violence. Even though your culturally different partner may be on his best behavior, take note of what happens when the two of you have a dispute or disagreement. Does he clam up and then take it out on you later? Or does he blow up at you? Does he walk away in a huff? You may even mention that you heard that many women in his culture have been victims of physical violence. Get his reaction to that statement. Watch his body language. Listen to what he says. If he says that they were beaten because they deserved it or they were too outspoken or they disobeyed their husband, that's a serious red flag.

CHAPTER 12

Lethal Toxic Mate Combinations

Recognizing Toxic Traits in Yourself

Some women are startled to recognize themselves in the profiles listed in Chapter 2. If that happened to you, it can be upsetting. But it's a fact—while this book focuses on Toxic Men, it is essential to note that women can be toxic as well. If you see yourself in any of these toxic categories, it may be a blessing in disguise. Because you have recognized these toxic traits in yourself, you can do something about them if you choose. You have completed the most difficult task, which is to objectively look at yourself and see your toxic flaws. You can now seek professional guidance to help you modify your toxic behaviors or you can monitor them yourself. Or you can choose to live with these traits.

Even if you have toxic traits, it depends on what traits your mate has that will determine whether or not you can coexist in a harmonious manner. For example, a Selfish Me-Myself-and-I Narcissist can maintain a long relationship with an Instigating Backstabbing Meddler. Since the Selfish Me-Myself-and-I Narcissist is only concerned with himself and his business and since the Instigating Backstabbing Meddler is only concerned with the Narcissist and their his business, the two of them have a lot in common. They are both completely focused on the Selfish Me-Myself-and-I Narcissist. The Narcissist may even welcome the intrusion and some of the backstabbing, as long as it focuses on his major concern—himself. I have personally seen this toxic combination of a couple, and they have been married for fifty years. The Narcissist loves himself and loves and appreciates his Meddler wife for all the attention she pays him by meddling in his affairs. The Meddler wife in turn loves and appreciates her husband because he adores it when she gets into his business, thereby making him feel that the world revolves around him. She immerses herself in his life, from the color of his tie to whether he had a good bowel movement that day. Each of them satisfies his or her own need as well as the other's.

Six Sick and Dangerous Combinations

Though some combinations of personality types can mesh relatively well, others are just the opposite. Because of the particular attributes of each type, the combination—whether in a personal relationship or a business collaboration—can be especially volatile and dangerous. These couplings are:

1. The Angry Bullying Control Freak and the Sneaky Passive-Aggressive Silent-but-Deadly Erupting Volcano
2. The Angry Bullying Control Freak and Another Angry Bullying Control Freak
3. The Selfish Me-Myself-and-I Narcissist and the Emotional Refrigerator
4. The Wishy-Washy Spineless Wimp and the Arrogant Self-Righteous Know-It-All
5. The Selfish Me-Myself-and-I Narcissist and the Seductive Manipulative Cheating Liar
6. The Socio-Psychopath and Anyone

These six combinations are so dangerous that they often result in physical harm or even death. So forewarned is forearmed! Read on for more specific information.

1. The Angry Bullying Control Freak and the Sneaky Passive-Aggressive Silent-but-Deadly Erupting Volcano

Someone with a very strong, explosive personality who has a tendency to boss and control another is a horrible match for a person who quietly keeps things in and harbors ill feelings until she has finally had enough and ends up exploding emotionally. They can both become so vindictive that they end up destroying both their lives.

We have all seen a real-life combination of these two types: Jon and Kate Gosselin, the parents of sextuplets and twin daughters and stars of the reality show *Jon and Kate Plus 8*. Jon, the Sneaky Passive-Aggressive Silent-but-Deadly Erupting Volcano, went on ABC's *20/20* and told interviewer Chris Cuomo that he despised Kate. Kate, in turn, went on *The View* and complained about how Jon hooked up with the babysitter, and on other television shows telling how he took the family's finances out of their joint account. On and on it went. But how did things get to this point? One only has to watch the show to find out.

Kate was a self-described control freak. She couldn't get along with anyone. She was bossy and not very loving or affectionate to Jon. In fact, we saw how she emotionally and even physically continued to abuse him on the show. She cut him down in front of the kids, yelled at him, and was always irritated and annoyed at him when he didn't do things exactly her way.

Jon took it and took it and said nothing. But as the show progressed, you could see Jon's passive-aggressiveness begin to emerge. He began making mocking facial expressions and snide remarks under his breath. Finally, the couple announced their breakup. Jon admitted during his media war with Kate that he was indeed passive-aggressive. That is no doubt the reason why he acted out as he did. He was twenty-two when they first married and had eight kids by the time he was twenty-seven. Leaving his job, he became a househusband, while Kate was traveling around the country doing lectures. He wanted to live too! But instead of communicating his needs, he started having affairs with many young women and acted irresponsibly.

The moral of the story is that no Angry Bullying Control Freak should ever be with a Sneaky Passive-Aggressive Silent-but-Deadly Erupting Volcano because when the emotional volcano finally erupts, and the bully has gone too far in her disrespect for the Volcano by not listening to him and trying to control him through anger and abuse, the results can be devastating.

2. The Angry Bullying Control Freak and Another Angry Bullying Control Freak

Two Angry Bullying Control Freaks vying for power in the relationship, personal or professional, is deadly. In a professional situation, these like personalities will never accomplish anything or be productive unless one of them becomes more flexible. If neither of them bends, there will be a stalemate and nothing will get accomplished. They will be frustrated with each another and it will never work.

For example, Becca was an actress with a very strong personality. Sid, her manager, had a very similar headstrong personality. Becca wanted to go one way with her career and Sid wanted it to go another way. Needless to say, the clashes were intense, resulting in frequent shouting matches. They were both miserable and frustrated because neither of them did what the other wanted. They could never see eye to eye with one another, so they soon ended up parting ways.

In a personal relationship, these two Toxic Types may not find it as easy to end their relationship so soon. Partners often stay together because this tumultuous relationship—with all its heated emotion of screaming, yelling, and fighting—often elicits passion as a byproduct. These emotions are translated into passionate sex. So there is a push-pull. They can't get along, so they fight . . . but after they fight, the makeup sex is great. Still, this emotional roller coaster ride can only last so long. One can't keep going through the ups and downs without it taking a toll on the relationship. After a while, there is no makeup sex because the fights and the disagreements are too traumatic.

3. The Selfish Me-Myself-and-I Narcissist and the Emotional Refrigerator

If you put a Selfish Me-Myself-and-I Narcissist with an Emotional Refrigerator, the relationship will not work. The Narcissist will act out to get the Emotional Refrigerator's attention. However, the Emotional Refrigerator will continue to ignore his or her mate, and not provide the constant attention that the Narcissist needs to exist.

The more emotional and reactive the Narcissist becomes, the more turned off the Emotional Refrigerator gets. This is a particularly dangerous and lethal combination because the Narcissist can go to such extremes as to even get violent with the Emotional Refrigerator, just to get some type of reaction from him or her.

Since Narcissists are so self-consumed and think everyone loves and adores them as much as they love and adore themselves, they have no clue that Emotional Refrigerators often doesn't feel the same way about them until it is too late.

Tina knew that her new boyfriend Marty was a bit on the quiet side, but she thought nothing of it. She minimized his annoyance at her for her public displays of affection. She thought that because he was such a great lover in the bedroom, she could eventually "train" him to be more lovey-dovey out of the bedroom, especially in public. She showed me a photo of the two of them in which she was leaning over to kiss him, but his face looked scrunched up, his head was leaning away from her, and there was a stiffness in his posture, reflecting the muscle tension in his body. He seemed to be pulling away from her. I also noticed how his right hand was cupped into a fist and that his toes were pointed in the opposite direction. This indicated that he did not like what she was doing and wanted to get away from her. While she thought it was a "cute" photo, I read the photo as being anything but cute. I told her that her man didn't seem very happy. She dismissed it by telling me she'd make him come around to liking her public hugs and kisses.

One day she was in a restaurant doing her lovey-doveying and making him cringe. He told her several times to stop it. Finally, he pushed her off of him with such an angry force that she landed on the floor. Needless to say, that was the end of their relationship.

This toxic combination is often seen in the workplace when there is a nonemotional boss or coworker and a narcissist. The Narcissist will seek attention while the Refrigerator will ignore him. The harder the Narcissist tries, the more resolutely the Refrigerator will ignore. There is only frustration and anger unless the two of them "know before whom they stand," as the Old Testament says. so they can modify their behavior and always act professionally.

4. The Wishy-Washy Spineless Wimp and the Arrogant Self-Righteous Know-It-All

This toxic combination is one of the most common and one of the most lethal. It is typically seen when a woman who is young, timid, afraid to do anything wrong, unable to stick up for herself, insecure, helpless, and dependent marries a man who is bright, successful, all-knowing, overly self-confident, and a take-charge type, and who either has a lot of potential or is already financially set. It is the typical Cinderella, Sleeping Beauty, Snow White Syndrome, where the handsome prince rescues the insecure damsel and brings her into his awesome world.

This happened to Betty Bisceglia. She was a beautiful young woman from a working-class family who married a man from the upper middle class, Dan Broderick. She helped him through medical school and had his children. When he decided to go to law school, she helped by holding down several jobs. She followed him to San Diego, raised his children, kept a beautiful home for him, and accompanied him to social functions to help him build his new business. She gave up everything for him and was one hundred percent devoted to him.

Suddenly her lifeline was cut when he abruptly left her for a twenty-something stewardess. He coldly left Betty without an explanation and gave her a meager divorce settlement from the multimillions she believed she helped him earn due to the sacrifices she made. After the divorce, Betty shot and killed him and his stewardess mistress, who had subsequently became his wife. She now sits in prison for perhaps the rest of her life.

According to psychologists, Betty had an extreme dependence on her husband. She desperately needed his approval because she never established her own identity. Without his approval, she had even less of an identity. So she sought to destroy the person who was the sole reason for her existence. She spinelessly dedicated her life to this man who "knew it all," and made all of her decisions. When he made the decision that she would no longer be in his life, she made the terrible decision to end his, instead of moving on with hers.

If you invest your entire being in a man and then he flicks you away as if he is flicking away ash from a cigarette, with no regard or respect for you, you will feel lost and desperate. If you feel you have no options or that your life has essentially been taken from you, you'll realize that you have given up your life for nothing. And if you feel desperate, angry, and as if you have nothing left to lose, you may resort to drastic, desperate measures. Avoid this situation by maintaining your own identity and control over your own life.

5. The Selfish Me-Myself-and-I Narcissist and the Seductive Manipulative Cheating Liar

When someone is self-centered, he believes the world revolves around him. So if he is given the ultimate slap in the face by being cheated on by his Seductive Manipulative Cheating Liar partner, the results can be tragic. This personality duo often ends with one of the parties committing a "crime of passion," which is most often the result when infidelity occurs. But it can also occur when one party feels slighted, manipulated, or as if he or she has been taken advantage of in any way.

For example, Bonita, a Latin beauty, made sure everyone noticed her by wearing revealing outfits to show off her sexy figure. Since childhood, everyone—including her rich husband, Bernardo, a successful land developer—catered to her because of her extraordinary beauty.

Bernardo showered her with everything her heart desired, which fed her already swollen ego. Bonita was all about Bonita and spent most of her day lunching, getting massages, shopping, or being catered to by her household staff. At night, she accompanied her husband to social events, always looking glamorous. One night at a dinner party, he left the table and told her he would be right back. Too much time passed, so she went to find him to tell him she wanted to leave. She found him having sex with someone by the pool. She immediately ran over to him, picked up a huge planter, and smashed him over the head with it. He ended up in a coma.

There are countless other examples of a person's narcissistic ego being so shattered that it clouds his or her judgment to the point he or she reacts with an uncontrolled sudden burst of violence to a perceived ultimate betrayal.

6. The Socio-Psychopath and Anyone

Go back to page 48 and reread the profile for the Socio-Psychopath. Memorize it. If you encounter anyone with those traits, immediately end your relationship with the person. Don't play games with the Socio-Psychopath. You will never win and it could cost you your life.

Things never change with a Socio-Psychopath, no matter how rich, powerful, or famous he or she is. However, when a Socio-Psychopath is powerful, rich, and famous, it can be blinding. People often refuse to accept that someone so powerful, rich, and famous could be this type of person. But if you keep your head in the sand, you're only risking your physical, emotional, and financial well-being.

While Socio-Psychopaths may be able to fool you for a while, they really can't maintain healthy personal or business relationships because their behavioral and personality deficiencies eventually catch up with them, often with tragic results. For example, Scott Peterson fooled a lot of people for a long time, including his in-laws and his wife, Lacy. Today, he sits on death row in San Quentin prison, awaiting his fate for killing his then-pregnant wife and their unborn son.

CHAPTER 13

Detecting Toxic Men Online

Analyzing Toxicity from the Written Word

With online dating services, social networking sites, and online communities being a big part of our daily lives, it is essential that you know with whom you are communicating across cyberspace. You need to know who is real and who isn't, whom you can and cannot trust. Just as you can read a lot about a man from his voice and speech signals and facial and body language, you can learn a lot about a man over the Internet from his writing signals.

Because the Internet affords such anonymity, it gives people the opportunity to be who they want to be, not who they really are. Its very nature lends itself to attracting many people who may not be as forthright as you are. Since you can't see or hear them, you have to rely on scrutiny of the written word to determine whether or not they're telling the truth.

In general, use common sense. If you read a dating profile that sounds full of exaggerations or amazing claims, chances are it is not true. It's about as likely to be true as an e-mail from Nigeria telling you your lost relative left you a million dollars, and all you have to do is provide them with your banking information to get the money. If it sounds too good to be true, it is.

As you communicate online, look for consistency while chatting back and forth. If a potential dating partner is typing one thing initially and something drastically different a while later, something is wrong—for example, sharing that he has no kids when you first begin corresponding and then, weeks later, he lets you know that he has to take his son to a

Little League game. That's a huge red flag. If you observe it, ask deeper questions or bring it to his attention and watch for his response. See whether he addresses it head on or gives you a convoluted and overly wordy explanation. If you see variations in his story, he's trying to cover up something.

Also, if he seems excessively private or too stingy with revealing information, that also indicates that he has something to hide. If you write questions and he is evasive or writes back curt answers, it is a big tell that he's not being honest.

Red Flags

When you observe communication red flags, you can be sure that something is not right. Anyone who is not being open and forthright is not worth getting to know. His nondisclosure game usually means that he has something to hide. Therefore, you don't need to spend your time and effort to discover the truth. Following are other signs that the person you're communicating with online may have some toxic traits.

RAMPANT MISSPELLINGS

If the material you see is *full* of misspellings, he may be a person who is always in hurry or who has a short attention span and isn't taking the time to spellcheck. To him, getting the message out is more important than getting it out accurately. It may also reflect a tendency to be careless, a lack of diligence, or impulsiveness. If these traits are personally toxic to you, then you may not want to pursue your online communication any further.

On the other hand, don't be too hasty in your assessment. Some of us are terrible spellers! Many out there in cyberspace have learning disabilities such as dyslexia, which impairs their spelling. You should ask questions about their spelling and why they have so many spelling errors before you jump to any conclusion that they may be toxic to you.

OVERUSE OF CYBER LINGO AND ABBREVIATIONS

If there is a lot of lingo and slang (that you may or may not understand) in his e-mails, it can be a sign that he is of a different generation (probably younger than you). That may be a good thing or a bad thing, depending on what you are looking for. It could be good, for instance, if you are also of the generation that uses that particular lingo.

If you don't understand the lingo, that is a bad thing, because it reflects that you two are not "speaking" the same language. He may also use a lot of abbreviations that you may not be familiar with. If that's the case, it could cause a problem in your communication, especially since texting jargon changes so rapidly. You would have to memorize the latest alphabet soup just to keep up with him, which you may find to be too much effort.

LENGTHY CORRESPONDENCE

If he's long-winded on the keyboard in his responses, it means he either has lot to say to you or he has a lot of time on his hands. If he does a free-flow stream-of-consciousness, you can pick up a lot from it. It may reveal his state of mind, what he wants from you, or some of his unintentionally revealed secrets.

FEW WORDS

Conversely, a man of few keystrokes with minimal responses may have little to say to you. He may also be doing several things at once, like e-mailing you, instant-messaging someone else, and watching something on YouTube or television. This may not only reflect his inability to focus, but also be an indicator of his interest in you.

BAD GRAMMAR

It's one thing if his spelling is bad, but it is another thing if his grammar is bad. You need to know why. It could mean that he is not well educated or he does not have a very good command of the language, or that the language in which he's corresponding to you is not his native language. It may also mean nothing—that he is writing as he would speak, without paying attention to grammatical rules.

IF HE DOESN'T WITHHOLD ANYTHING

If he writes too much personal and intimate information, he often has problems with boundaries and judgment. He is not too discriminating. You could very well be anyone, including his journal or his diary. Too often, people tell way too much over the Internet. They often write as a stream of consciousness. Because they are in the comfort of their own space, many feel more freedom to blurt out whatever is on their mind without a second thought.

If he does this, pay careful attention to what he writes, because it may give you a lot of insight as to who he is.

Picking Up Toxic "Tells" from an Online Profile

When reading profiles on Internet dating and social networking sites, look especially carefully at (a) his moniker—the name he selected for himself, (b) his photos—pictures revealing information about who he really is, and (c) the content of all areas of his profile.

If you remember the important hints I will share with you in the rest of this chapter, you will know whether to hit the delete button or take it to the next level.

TOXIC MONIKERS

A man's moniker, the name he selects to describe how he sees himself or wants to be seen, speaks volumes about him. This is the username he has on a site. It tells you what really matters to him. The name can reflect his passions ("filmfan"), interests ("travelman"), activities ("hockyjocky"), sexuality ("hungman"), what he's looking for ("peacefuliving"), what he values ("outdoordude"), and most importantly, how he feel about himself ("happyhal" or "dumb1"). But if you read something like eviledevil666 or lucifer8u, don't answer unless you're in a similar mindset.

A man's moniker may also have sexual undertones that tell you exactly what fetishes he is looking for. Again, don't respond unless you are like-minded. Also, pay attention to monikers that are plays on words, like "masterbeater" or "beaverfriendly" or "pussiluvr8," as that may be their intention for seeking out a date. Men who use sexually explicit monikers on a nonsexual site are showing inappropriate behavior and poor judgment. These toxic traits may often surface in other situations in his life. This is a definite red flag in terms of the potential of his being toxic.

The number 007 or James Bond references on dating sites are plentiful. They tell you about the man's fantasy life or how he would like to see himself—as an invincible ladies' man. If this is not the type of man you are looking for, skip the 007 James Bond wannabes.

If you're concerned about what he means by his moniker, don't be shy about asking him. If he responds with something that is not your cup of tea, you don't have to go any further.

TOXIC PHOTOS

You can learn a tremendous amount of information from a man's photo, such as what matters to him (if he is with his kids, a boat, a skateboard), his self-esteem or lack thereof (ramrod posture, usually indicating that he is a rigid uptight kind of guy or slumped-over hunched shoulders, usually indicating that he lacks self-esteem), and grooming and neatness (or lack thereof, if he has greasy hair and is in a sloppy environment). Keep in mind the following questions as you check out his photos:

- *Does he have good hygiene and fashion sense?* Carefully examine a man's grooming and clothing. Is he stylish or way too casual for your tastes? Is he a fashion misfit who would drive you nuts because he is so unaware of how to dress? Is he wearing a sweat-stained shirt? If he is, you might wonder why he isn't putting his best foot forward in such a public first impression.

- *Is the photo extremely old?* Look for clues in the hair and clothing style or background of the photo that can tell you if it's a dated photo of him.
- *Are his kids in the pictures?* When a man includes his kids in his photos, he's telling you that his kids are a priority and are part of the package if you become involved with him. But if he has tons of photos of them, it usually means that he has absolutely no room for you in his life. You would be an intruder, as his life seems to be complete with just him and his kids. Showing lots of photos of his kids also lets you know that you had better like his kids and get along with them; otherwise, you are out. Having lots of his kids' photos on a dating site also shows that he has poor judgment. Besides being an invasion of their privacy, the kids aren't dating you, he is. So there is no reason why a ten-year-old boy's or a thirteen-year-old girl's face should be plastered on a singles' site!
- *Are his dogs in all his photos?* The same holds true if there are countless photos of him and his dogs. One photo is enough. If there are too many, the dog will probably get more attention than you. If the dog should growl at you, forget about the relationship.
- *Is he holding an infant in any pictures?* Some men show photos of themselves holding an infant or a toddler. If a child is that young and the child is his, you have to question the character of any man who would leave a woman who recently gave birth. But the reality is that when you see a man with a very young baby in the photo with him, the child is usually not his. It is often a friend's or relative's baby. He is trying to appeal to women who like or want babies. He knows quite well that women of childbearing age are often looking for a man to father their children. So, this is his way of attracting more women by letting them know that he could possibly be their "baby daddy."
- *Are photos missing altogether?* If there is no photo at all, forget him. He may have something to hide. He's not playing fair, because the

rules are that everyone shows a photo. If he is high profile personality (such as, in local politics or a high-ranking businessman) and doesn't want a photo shown publicly, then he needs to find another way to date.

- *Does he appear to be hiding anything?* Even if he is in a photo where it is a sunny day or he is at the beach, if he is wearing sunglasses, he may have something to hide—such as his identity. The point of posting a photo is so a potential date can see exactly what you look like and who you are. If a man is disguised, you should also be concerned. If he appears in sunglasses or is in a photo where you only see part of his face, he may not want to reveal how he looks because in many cases, he may be married or involved with someone else. If he is standing next to someone who has been cropped out of the photo, the person who was cropped out may have been a friend, relative, or coworker. But it could also have been his wife or girlfriend.

- *Has he posted a million pictures?* If a man posts more than ten photos of himself, he may be narcissistic. The more photos he displays, the more narcissistic he probably is.

- *Does he appear to be trying to be someone else?* Louis was a boring businessman but wanted women to think he was a daring professional racecar driver, which he was not. So he posted countless photos of himself dressed up in racing gear standing next to a Ferrari. It reflected what he wanted to be, not who he really was. When the various women he met asked if they could see his racecar or asked more probing questions about his Ferrari, who his sponsors were, his fears on the track, where he raced, or if he ever got injured racing, they quickly discovered that he was a phony. They usually cut the date short and never returned any of his subsequent calls. They felt that if he could give a false impression that he was a racecar driver, there was no telling what else he would lie about.

- *Are there other women in his photos?* There is nothing more unnerving than when a man posts a photo of himself next to a beautiful woman. After all, these men are on a dating site to meet women, and no woman wants to see other women standing next to a man they may find appealing. Subconsciously, these men put up the photo as a barometer for you. They are saying, "If you aren't as pretty as the lady in this photo, don't even bother." The bottom line is that it shows a man's insensitivity and poor judgment.

- *Is he half-naked?* When men wear only a towel or are shirtless, they are trying to convey their sexuality to you and to let you know that this is one of the main reasons they are on the site.

- *Is he too goofy for you?* Watch for wacky pictures, like one where he's fitting a whole orange or his entire fist in his mouth or wearing a coconut bra. If you think it's funny and that's your sense of humor, go for it. If not, click Next.

- *Does he look creepy?* Finally, if you look at his photo and it gives you a chill in a bad way, don't even think of contacting him. If he has crazy eyes or a sinister smile or a masklike grin and it causes you to wonder, trust your instincts. However, keep in mind that not all serial killers look like serial killers. After all, Ted Bundy was as handsome as any Hollywood actor. But if something in the photo doesn't sit right with you, your limbic system is speaking to you. Listen carefully and move on.

TOXIC WRITTEN WORDS

If a guy sounds vague in his written profile, he probably has something to hide, such as a marriage. What he doesn't say is just as revealing as what he does say. If he leaves large blanks, especially about his work, he may be hiding the fact that he is jobless or penniless. If he leaves blanks about his interests, he may be too lazy or not serious about connecting with others.

Since men are more visual than women and often focused on the physical, women must pay close attention to the part of the profile where a man talks about the body type to which he is attracted. If he says he likes thin or athletic women, and you are curvy or a bit on the chunky side, forget about it. You can never change his mind, because, as we discussed in Chapter 5, he is imprinted and knows what he wants. If you decide to meet him in person anyway, rest assured he won't make you feel very welcome. Better to read this part carefully so neither of you will waste the other's time or create ill feelings.

The same holds true for the part about kids. If he wants them and you don't or he doesn't want them and you do, take him at his word. Don't think you will convert him to your point of view. Only aggravation can come out of getting started with a man who is on a different path than you.

Warning Signs of Toxic Men in Cyberspace

In paying close attention to what is on a man's profile or e-mails he writes you, especially in the online dating and social world, you will learn a tremendous amount about him. You will be able to discern whether he is arrogant, snobby, sarcastic, insensitive, superficial, lazy, or impatient, and whether he is mentally or physically ill. You can also tell a lot about a man's toxic personality traits by reading between the lines. What he says in the written arena is just as crucial as what he says in the verbal and nonverbal arena. I will share with you some actual excerpts from profiles as well as correspondence so that you can be on the lookout for these Toxic Types in cyberspace.

HE'S CHEAP OR HAS MONEY ISSUES

If the man constantly refers to finances and frugality, something is amiss. He either has no money or is thinking of a way to scam you for money. Here are some excerpts of a dating profile where the man mentions his frugality way too many times throughout the profile, indicating that there are definitely monetary concerns.

"On Saturday mornings, I shop for groceries and pay $30 instead of $100 with the newspaper coupons. It tells me I'm not stupid."

"I prefer to meet for coffee or breakfast, something light. And don't get it wrong, I'm not cheap at all."

Be sure to read a guy's whole profile to look for how often he mentions a specific issue, which indicates it is of great concern to him. In this day and age, most of us have financial concerns and think of ways to be more frugal. But if a man is always bringing up his financial issues, they may be seriously affecting his life, which would in turn affect your life, if you end up with him. By constantly referring to his finances, he may be telling you that he can't afford to take you out, pay for dates, or buy you gifts, especially expensive ones.

HE'S A BAD BOY

If he verbally says to you he's a "bad boy," believe him. Similarly, if he puts it in writing that he's a "bad boy" (via an e-mail or dating profile), also believe him. If you ignore it, don't be surprised when you find out he cheated on you. Here is an actual excerpt from a profile letting you know that he is bad. He is putting out a challenge to you that you will never be able to meet—you will never tame him.

"I'm a bad boy—a really bad boy. But for the right woman who can tame me I might not be that bad."

HE'S NONCOMMITTAL

If a man writes that he isn't looking to "jump into marriage," that means he is looking for a date or a good time, not a relationship that could lead to a full-time commitment. Here is an excerpt where the man lets you know that he doesn't want to be pushed into marriage. So if you think you can change his mind, you better move on.

"I'd like a relationship but not looking to jump into marriage or anything like that. I'd like to go slow and see where it goes. I'm definitely not pushy

nor do I try to exert my will on anyone. You'll either like me or not and I'm not going to change that by anything I do."

Even though he doesn't *say* he's anti-marriage, that's what he means. What appears to be his caution in saying "Let's take it slow and see where it goes" actually means that he's noncommittal and that he may never want to commit in the long run. His statement may also speak volumes about his fear of intimacy. He hasn't even met the woman yet and he is already setting limits on any potential relationship. This is not something he needs to put in a profile, but rather something he needs to say after he had met the woman and started to date her. Just as I cautioned you earlier in this book to be aware of men who want to marry you quickly, I caution you about men who hold up barriers and relationship limits before they have even met you. It says they may only be interested in dating you, but not exclusively. It also lets you know that marrying you is out of the question.

You should, of course, take into account his age—a twenty-year-old may only be concerned with dating, not marriage, at that point in his life.

HE'S AN ARROGANT CONTROL FREAK

These men will verbally attack you because they have a preconceived notion of how *they* want you to do and be. They are angry and delight in putting you down. They have chips on their shoulders and anger toward women, beginning with the one that initially rejected them. It's usually their way or the highway. They want to run the show and gain control right away. That is why they will often tear you down so they can get the upper hand. Here is an excerpt from a profile that indicates the man is like this:

"I'm pretty much an A-plus personality and I like to be in control of things. I'm a real man and I believe a real man has to take control and not be a wuss."

Here is an actual e-mail he wrote to show his interest in a woman whose profile he came across. Note the immediate hostility and trying to put her down so that he can gain control as he tries to put the woman on the defensive.

"I saw your picture and thought you looked beautiful, but that dress has gotta go. You look like a schoolteacher. It doesn't make you look as sexy as I know you probably are."

Notice how he uses intermittent reinforcement to try to gain her interest. He gives a compliment with one hand and takes it away with the next, gives another one, and then takes it back. Getting involved with a control freak like this could be a real roller coaster ride.

He may also try to gain an edge over you by arrogantly criticizing your spelling or your grammar as this control freak did: *"you said you read books 'written by people whoM I admire.' Can't resist a good 'whom'?"*

HE'S ONLY INTERESTED IN SEX

There are countless sex sites out there that cater to every sexual need, so if a man hints at sexual undertones in his general dating profile or in your correspondence with him, it should raise a red flag—he should be on one of those sites if those are his interests. While flirtation and some sexy undertones are appealing, this man's only interest is getting any woman into bed.

He will tint everything with a sexual undertone. If he's sexing you up with the written word before he even meets you, know that you are not the only one with whom he is doing this. For him, it's a numbers game as to who will respond. As soon as someone does, he's succeeded.

It is also not uncommon to hear sexually provocative comments if he gets you on the phone, such as asking you in a seductive voice what you're wearing, or how he touched himself looking at your photo, or how you turn him on. He doesn't even know anything about you—nor does he want to. For this type of toxic cyber character, cybersex or phone sex with you is foremost on his mind. He wants to see if he can seduce you into a sexual liaison. So, if you hear early sex talk too soon, hang up or tell him he's on the wrong site. It's disrespectful and you need to let him know that right away, unless you are like-minded.

HE'S A NARCISSIST

These men only know the words *I*, *me*, and *my*. To them, your only value is being on the other end of the computer, receiving the information that is *all* about them. They rarely ask anything about you unless it pertains directly back to them. When you see a lot of "I's" in their profile or in their e-mail correspondence to you, pay attention. When little attention or feedback is given to you and no questions are asked about you, know you're most likely corresponding with a person who really loves himself more than he could ever love anyone else—a narcissist.

HE'S A GUILTER

There are also those who try to make you feel bad for not responding or not responding to them quickly enough. If they don't even know you and feel slighted by you, just think what can happen if you have some sort of relationship with them. Here is an excerpt of a man trying to guilt someone for not responding sooner.

> *"Thanks for winking back, I think. . . . I winked and wrote you about two weeks ago. . . So thanks for FINALLY answering . . . must have been reeel busy if you took so long to answer!"*

Unfortunately, too many women fall for the cyber guilters, guilting them into responding and even into a relationship. Because they "don't want to hurt the man's feelings," or they are so concerned with what he may think and want to be liked, they respond. This is a huge red flag. When a man admonishes you before he even knows you, just think of what he will do when he *does* know you. So whenever you see someone laying a guilt trip on you, hit the delete button.

HE ACTS LIKE A VICTIM

This Toxic Man will make negative statements about himself, revealing how powerless he feels and how low his self-esteem has plummeted so that you will feel sorry for him and save him by selecting him. Here is an excerpt of a profile from such a cyber victim:

NOW on the off chance there is actually a woman on the site who would be interested in meeting a really nice guy, here I am but I am not sure anyone will give me a chance. I am loyal and loving and you would really like me if you knew me, but I guess there are too many other guys out there for you to give me a decent chance. the "ball is in YOUR court" . . . :)

What a turnoff! It smacks of desperation and a loser.

HE ACTS CREEPY

Just as there are photos that may give you a sense something is wrong, you may see profiles or e-mails that don't sit well with you after you read them. Pay close attention to your visceral sense that something is not right. While a man may initially show charm and glibness, he will eventually reveal his penchant for the violent and the macabre if he really is mentally disturbed.

If someone writes an e-mail describing fetishes or mentions necrophilia, report him on the "contact" or "concerns" section of the dating or matchmaking website. Then delete and block him forever. If he has any of your other e-mail addresses or phone numbers and continues to contact you after you have told him not to do so, call the police. If he threatens you, contact the FBI's cybercrime unit.

Dater Beware!

Even though there are many disturbed men out there who prey on women online, it certainly is possible to meet a nice guy online. However, you have to be very careful and even more vigilant than you would be in person, since guys can lie online so much easier. They feel that they can be anyone they choose to be and you will never know the difference. That is why it is essential to pay close attention to all the signs of toxic behavior that were discussed in this chapter.

PART IV

How to Deal with a Toxic Man

CHAPTER 14

Effective Techniques for Specific Types of Toxic Men

One Method That Doesn't Work: Trying to Change Him!

Toxic Men are here to stay. They have been around since the beginning of time and will be here until the end of time. Just as you cannot change a tiger's stripes, you can never change a Toxic Man.

Too many women make the fatal mistake of being aware of a man's toxicity and ignoring it. Whether subconsciously or consciously, they decide to take on this Toxic Man like a huge project and change him. They think that they will clean up his mean temper, his stinginess, his arrogance, his cheating, his drug addiction or drinking, and his lying ways, and everything will be fine. If you have been guilty of trying to fix a Toxic Man, you are not alone. Millions of women think the exact same way.

Yet there is nothing whatsoever you can do to change a man! While you may perhaps see a hint of change or even a dramatic change in your Toxic Man, it will only last a short time. It cannot be sustained. As far as men are concerned, there is no such thing as a "fixer-upper." With a fixer-upper house, you can easily throw on a new coat of paint and make some superficial changes to improve how it looks. But the foundation and pipes also need complicated repair jobs done by a professional in order to fully function. Similarly, while you can change a man's clothing or hairstyle, drag him to the ballet, or get him to change some of his toxic ways for a while, you need professional assistance to make a lasting difference. Change will only stick if he wants to change. Otherwise, you are wasting your precious time.

It has been my experience during many years of seeing clients that if change is to occur, it must be initiated by the man himself, not by anyone else. The man has to want to change for himself and not because someone forces him to do so. He needs to realize on his own that it is his toxic behavior that is hurting him as well as others he loves. When men finally realize that what they are doing isn't working and will never work, that is the only time change can take place. Change has to come from him directly, not from your wanting him to change or giving him ultimatums. I can't stress this enough: You cannot help him change *unless he wants to change.* The impetus for his reformation has to be his own realizations or desires or frustrations.

EVEN IF YOU'VE CHANGED SOMETHING BEFORE, DON'T TRY TO CHANGE A TOXIC MAN!

So many of you who are reading this probably think of yourself as a nurturing, loving, special, confident, strong, gutsy woman or a woman who has worked miracles in your professional or personal lives by turning others, perhaps including your own children, around. So you think, "I've turned other things around in my life—my finances, my job, my weight—so I can certainly turn a Toxic Man around."

If you happen to be in a helping or nurturing profession—a psychologist, a nurse, a doctor, a teacher, a professor—or in any service industry, you are even more prone to feeling this way. If you happen to be a mother, your entire life is all about helping, nurturing, and turning things around. So how difficult can it be to apply the same principles to your man?

It is impossible. You cannot apply what you do in your professional life to your personal life when it comes to a man.

Effective Techniques to Use with Specific Types of Toxic Men

Whether the Toxic Man in your life is a date, spouse, father, brother, neighbor, boss, employee, or coworker, it's probably difficult to erase him from your life forever for a number of reasons, from financial concerns to how you were raised. Since many women are stuck to some degree with a Toxic Man, I have developed ten tried-and-true techniques that have effectively helped millions of people around the world handle dysfunctional relationships. These strategies will help you manage your toxic relationship on a day-to-day basis. They are:

1. The Tension Blowout Let It Go Technique
2. The Extreme Tension Blowout Technique
3. The Change the Thought Technique
4. The Humor Technique
5. The Mirror Technique
6. The Direct Confrontation and Calm Questioning Technique
7. The Give Him Love and Kindness Technique
8. The Give Him Hell and Yell Technique
9. The Fantasy Technique
10. The Unplug Technique

Below you will learn about each of these ten techniques and which specific technique works on which specific types of Toxic Man.

1. The Tension Blowout Let It Go Technique
HOW IT WORKS

This technique helps you gain physical control over your emotions, serving as a vehicle to release tension by oxygenating yourself.

1. First, inhale a breath through your mouth for two seconds.
2. Think of the Toxic Man and what he said or did to you as you hold your breath for three seconds.
3. Keep thinking of him as you release him out of your psyche and your system as you gently, smoothly, and slowly blow him out on the exhaled breath of air. After you have done this, stop for two seconds without breathing.

Repeat these steps three times or as many times as you need to purge this Toxic Man from your psyche. Then breathe normally. If you feel lightheaded after you have exhaled so many times, take a seat and take slow, gentle, steady and smooth, rhythmic breaths as you calmly inhale and then exhale.

WHY IT WORKS

Using this technique allows you to quickly and easily release your anger and tension. The physical and symbolic action of breathing him out is very healing. Remember, as you inhale, don't symbolically breathe him back in with your thoughts. Instead, breathe in self-love and self-confidence. For example, think of all your assets and the great things about you as you inhale the good thoughts. Then as you exhale, switch and think of him and all the toxic things he has done. As you think of him, know that you are symbolically "letting him out of your life" on that exhaled breath.

TOXIC TYPES IT WORKS BEST FOR

The Tension Blowout Let It Go Technique works with *all* of the Toxic Types. It is the first place and fastest way you will find relief, so use it regularly to let out your tension around a Toxic Man. It is also relatively subtle and can be done anywhere in private or in public. You can do it in your car, on an elevator, in a store, at the office, and even in a business meeting. No one will even know what you are doing as you immediately begin to feel better.

2. The Extreme Tension Blowout Technique

HOW IT WORKS

This method is good for those private moments when you are alone, and when thoughts of his toxicity are really getting to you and the gentler Tension Blowout Technique is not working for you. The Extreme Blowout Technique can help you get rid of even more tension as well as the anger and anxiety you may be experiencing.

Note: If you have any history of medical or health issues, such as respiratory, circulatory, cardiac, or neurological conditions, and if you have ever been lightheaded or weak in the past, DO NOT attempt to do this exercise.

1. First, inhale a breath through your mouth for two seconds, just as you did in the Tension Blowout Technique.
2. Next, think of the Toxic Man and all of the toxic things that he has said or done to you as long as you have known him, as you hold your breath for three seconds.
3. Keep thinking of him and his toxic behaviors as you vigorously blow out the air with all of your strength. In essence, you are symbolically blowing every bit of him out of your psyche by forcefully blowing him out on the exhaled breath of air. After you have done this, stop for two seconds without breathing.

Now repeat these steps three times or as many times as needed to purge this Toxic Man from your psyche. Then breathe normally. You may discover that you feel lightheaded after you have exhaled so vigorously for many times. If so, take a seat and take slow rhythmic breaths as you calmly inhale and exhale and to regain your equilibrium. If you continue to feel lightheaded or weak, do not continue with this technique.

WHY IT WORKS

This technique works because it allows you to release all the anger and tension you're feeling about the Toxic Man in a healthy and safe way. It prevents you from keeping in those negative thoughts about him and having them churn around in your head, which can make you feel angrier and angrier.

It also provides you with a lot of immediate relief, because much of the tension will be gone as this technique oxygenates your entire system. After doing this technique, you will tend to feel not only more relaxed but more energized, as you have released ugly thoughts of him and the tension these toxic thoughts create within you. Once again, if you feel lightheaded, stop doing the technique immediately and do not continue! Sit down and rest until you gain your equilibrium. Always proceed with the caution as noted previously when doing or considering doing this exercise.

TOXIC TYPES IT WORKS BEST FOR

Extreme Tension Blowout Technique works with *all* of the Toxic Types, especially if your anger toward one of them is escalating. It provides you with an effective and healthy way to immediately release your tension, anger, and anxiety with regard to a Toxic Man.

3. The Change the Thought Technique

HOW IT WORKS

Sometimes you just can't seem to stop thinking of that Toxic Man, and he permeates every thought you have and every action you do. Often if you give yourself a suggestion or a verbal command such as "Stop the thought" or "Change the thought," it will allow you to change your thought pattern and think of something else.

As soon as the thought of the Toxic Man comes into your mind, immediately yell out as loud as you can at the moment, "Change the thought!" Then substitute that thought with something positive. Think of someone who has been good to you and supportive. Think of the best things that happened to you in your life. If you are at a loss for thoughts, make a list of everything in your life for which you are grateful. Keep that list with you at all times. In fact, make several copies of the list and keep one in your car and one in every room in your house. Keep a copy at work and in your purse. The bottom line is that you have it on hand to jog your memory into having a good thought instead of obsessing on negative thoughts of him. As you think of the positive things in your life, spend time saying a prayer and giving thanks for them.

WHY IT WORKS

The Change the Thought Technique works because you are substituting a positive thought for a negative one. You are training yourself to limit and eventually eliminate thinking and dwelling on the hurt that the

Toxic Man has caused you. It allows you to change your negative thinking and become more positive. It adds to and speeds up your healing process from the Toxic Man. It allows you to move on with your life and forces you to see that he is no longer the center of your universe.

TOXIC TYPES IT WORKS BEST FOR

This technique works best for any Toxic Man, especially those who have caused you extreme emotional and even physical pain. No matter how bad things may see, repeatedly looking at your gratitude list and thinking about it whenever the Toxic Man crosses your mind will show you that no matter how bad things got between the two of you, there are still things in your life that are more important and more meaningful than him. Changing the thought to a more positive one where you also give gratitude is the best antidote toward healing your emotional pain created by a Toxic Man.

4. The Humor Technique

HOW IT WORKS

Amusing yourself with humor is another way of dealing with a Toxic Man who makes toxic comments to you. It doesn't matter if anyone else thinks what you say is funny, as long as it gives you a chuckle. That is all that matters. If you can't think of anything humorous to say, get a joke book and memorize a few retorts you can say to a Toxic Man who cuts you down. For instance, you can say something like "I never forget a face, but in your case I'm willing to make an exception" or "Whatever's eating you must be suffering from food poisoning."

You can even deflect the humor onto yourself if you feel comfortable doing so. How can he cut you down if you've already humorously cut yourself down even more? It's difficult to be upset with someone who cuts herself down. One of my clients used this technique with a toxic boyfriend who tried to keep track of whatever she ate. After he asked, "Are you going to eat *another* piece of bread?" she looked at him, smiled, and said, "I sure am. This is just an appetizer because for the main course, I'm ordering a whole loaf of bread." He looked shocked as she giggled.

WHY IT WORKS

In essence, your goal is to fight fire with water, as his hostility is defused by your humor. Using this technique will also show him that you're "laughing off" his comment and not letting it affect you. It will show him that his comments don't have the negative impact on you that he thinks they have. As a result, you will notice that your response will often unnerve him and make him less likely to make a similar comment. It also allows you to take control of the situation and have the last word. After all, there is not much he can say after you have extinguished his intentionally hostile comment with humor.

TOXIC TYPES IT WORKS BEST FOR

Humor works with any toxic type, so try it on everyone in your personal and even in your professional life with the exception of Socio-Psychopaths, as they are often humorless. It works well with your boss, coworkers, or employees. It doesn't matter if they get angry or upset because the bottom line is that *you* are no longer feeling angry or upset. If they do happen to get angry or upset at your humorous retort, know that you have now regained control of the situation. Their anger gives you additional information as to how they really feel about you so, you know up front that they don't like you. Most commonly, you will see anger emerge with the Angry Bullying Control Freak, who needs to be in charge or have the last word, and the Selfish Me-Myself-and-I Narcissist, who is often humorless when it comes to looking at and laughing at himself. So if you use the Humor Technique around these types of toxic terrors, know that they may become even more toxic toward you. But there are Toxic Types on whom your humor may be more effective. Here are a couple of examples of how to use humor with certain Toxic Types.

The Jealous Competitor

Since the Jealous Competitor is into oneupmanship and topping whatever you say, as soon as he tries to top you, top him back, only this time make something up that sounds funny and outrageous. Let's say you tell him you are sore from your workout and he retorts with "Well

I'm more sore than you are. I bench-pressed three hundred pounds." You can then smile and reply, "I'm surprised because they say that you don't even feel the pain with the first three hundred pounds if you are really in shape." He's flustered and you have a giggle.

The Arrogant Self-Righteous Know-It-All

Since the Arrogant Self-Righteous Know-It-All seems to know everything, you can have a good laugh by asking him if he knows about some obscure subject. You can add your two cents to the topic with erroneous information that you make up. This will no doubt infuriate and make him squirm with discomfort.

He may start to talk at you, over you, or get even snottier in his behavior. You can just sit back and watch because you are, in essence, entertaining yourself. Keep interjecting some ridiculous or inaccurate information to watch him get even more flustered. As you chuckle at what's happening, you will find the tension leaving your body.

5. The Mirror Technique

HOW IT WORKS

This technique forces the man to see his behavior up close and personal as his toxic behavior is reflected back at him. That means if he yells, yell back. If he shouts, shout back. If he uses a gruff tone, use a gruff tone back at him. If he invades your space, invade his space right back. If he scowls at you, scowl right back at him.

Most of the time he will be shocked at your behavior and wonder why you are acting so horribly toward him. He may not have a clue about how he is treating you, as his inner hostility toward you compels him to act this way. But when he sees you acting that way, he will usually take personal offense. On the other hand, it may stop him in his tracks and he may even rethink his behavior. Still, there are other Toxic Men who may be acting toxic to you on purpose. He won't believe that you are actually calling him on his toxic behavior in such a bold and dramatic way and may continue to act as toxic as ever toward you.

WHY IT WORKS

The technique is very effective. If he directly confronts you as to why you are acting so hostile, you can tell him that you are just mirroring the exact way he has been treating you. If he doesn't ask or notice, you can feel free to bring it up. You can say "If you haven't noticed, I have been mirroring your toxic behavior."

When this technique is used, it sometimes puts a stop to the toxic behavior. Your mirroring often brings to the surface his subconscious attitudes and feeling about you. This realization often embarrasses him because you uncovered his hidden negative thoughts and feelings toward you. If he is conscious about what he has done to you, he will usually stop, because he'll realize that you won't put up with it and will instead give it right back to him.

TOXIC TYPES IT WORKS BEST FOR

Angry Bullying Control Freak

Sometimes mirroring the bully's behavior puts a stop to things. It certainly is worth a try. In the middle of one of his "mantrums," mirror him back and watch what happens. It's kind of like what happens when a baby hears another baby cry: the first baby stops crying. So will this big baby.

Selfish Me-Myself-and-I Narcissist

Mirroring also works with any man who talks about himself all the time. He definitely won't like it when the focus is off of him, so the more he talks about himself, the more you should interject about yourself. Eventually, he may get the message. If not, you will have to move on to another technique.

6. The Direct Confrontation and Calm Questioning Technique

HOW IT WORKS

In this technique, you directly tell him what he did and said and how it made you feel. This does not mean that you accuse him, because that can instigate a hostile reaction. You are simply stating facts—what was said and how it made you feel. You are clearly and openly letting him know that you will not be a victim.

The technique allows you to speak up for yourself. Do it in a way that is not whiny, hostile, or attacking. Instead, be direct and calm. When you speak up and say what is on your mind and how his behavior affected you, it not only causes him to respect you, it creates more self-respect. It allows you to set boundaries and let the man know what behaviors you will not accept.

Suppose he says something sarcastic or rude to you about eating a cupcake, such as "Are you sure you want to eat that? You know what they say—a second on the lips is forever on the hips." You can ask a question like "Why would it bother you that I am eating this cupcake? Do you think my hips are big?" In essence, you are asking him to tell you what he is really thinking and what he really means to say. Or you can ask "Are you saying that you think I am fat and that I will get fatter if I eat this cupcake and that you won't be attracted to me if I get fat?" Here your direct and bold questioning is putting him on the spot and forcing him to take accountability for his snide comment and be more direct.

You can also use the direct approach of telling him how it makes you feel when he says things like that to you. You can say, "When you make snide comments about what I eat, it hurts my feelings and shows me that you don't respect that I can make my own food choices. If I choose to eat a cupcake, that is my decision and I will deal with the consequences, if I think there are any. The bottom line is that I don't like it when you comment on my food when I am eating. I don't do it to you and I would like to have the same respect."

You can also set your boundaries by calmly questioning the man about why he feels he needs to speak to you the way he does, or what you did to offend him, that caused him to react so negatively.

WHY IT WORKS

This technique allows you to directly let him know that you are not pleased with his actions and how they have affected you. This usually opens up a dialogue, which is the first step to resolving your issue. When you confront him by questioning his toxic actions toward you, it may give him the opportunity to reveal why he may be harboring some hidden negative feelings about you. Perhaps it will get him to bring those negative feelings to the surface and explain why he is upset with something you said or did. You may even ask, "How would you react if I said or did this to you?" Or ask more general questions, such as "How do you think it makes a person feel when you say . . ." or "What do you think would cause someone to act with such hostility toward another person?" Being asked to explain and understand his own behavior can create an eye-opening experience for the Toxic Man.

TOXIC TYPES IT WORKS BEST FOR

The Direct Confrontation and Calm Questioning Technique works best with *all* the Toxic Types. No matter what his bad behavior, this strategy allows you to release your stress, communicate your concerns, and get to the bottom of solving the problem. Here are two types and the explanation of why the technique works for them.

Sneaky Passive-Aggressive Silent-but-Deadly Erupting Volcano

Since this type of Toxic Man is one of the most frightening types, you always need to check in with him, because you never know when he is going to verbally explode. Since he keeps things in and lets them fester until he has had enough, use this technique on a regular basis in order to get his thoughts and feelings out in the open. Check in with him by directly confronting how he makes you feel, or by questioning what he is feeling or to what he is acting or reacting.

The Angry Bullying Control Freak

If you are going to confront an Angry Bullying Control Freak, you need to do it in calm, nonargumentative tones. Often, your calmness will have a calming effect on *his* behavior. You don't want to put him on the defensive by saying "You did this to me" or "How dare you say such and such to me." If you accuse him, he won't hear a word you say. Instead, he'll be ready to fight back before you even finish your thought.

Instead, you need to put the focus on yourself and say how what he says affects you directly and how it makes you feel. This will allow him to hear things from your perspective so he doesn't automatically become defensive. Say something like "My feelings get really hurt when I'm yelled at" or "I really am more receptive when I'm spoken to in a kind tone." In calmly questioning and communicating with him, you are pursuing a line of logical and nonaccusatory behavior. That is the only way he will hear you. "What seems to be bothering you?" "How does it make you feel?" and "What can I do to make you not feel that way?" are other great questions to ask the Angry Bullying Control Freak.

In asking these types of questions, you are in control and are not a victim of his yelling and pushiness toward you. In using this technique, you are acting like the responsible adult and not like him—the tantrum-throwing child.

7. The Give Him Love and Kindness Technique
HOW IT WORKS
It takes a lot of inner fortitude and compassion to transform your anger into love and kindness toward a man who has been toxic to you. But if you consider that most Toxic Men suffer from a lack of love or attention in their early development, it may be easier for you to change your thinking. Sometimes the Christian precept of turning the other cheek may be the best thing to do if you want to make peace—even if it is also the *hardest* thing to do. Seeing things from the Toxic Man's point of view, and perhaps understanding his motivation for doing and saying what he has done and said, may possibly fill you with more compassion so that you let go of the anger and let out the love. I'm not saying that it is easy to do, but it is an available option.

In using this technique, visualize yourself as Mother Teresa or some other spiritual person you respect. Perhaps it's your priest, minister, rabbi, or imam. No matter how nasty your Toxic Man gets, you must be calm, use soothing tones, and keep a smile on your face and love in your heart.

Keep in mind just how much deep emotional pain this man must be in to act like he does.

You may even say "Know that even though you are acting like this, I still love you." Or you may say "Honey, you don't have to upset yourself." Use terms of endearment like "honey," "sweetheart," or "baby" along with your soothing tones, as these terms can help calm and diffuse the negativity and let him know that you still love and accept him.

WHY IT WORKS

It is amazing what the power of love can do. You may immediately see him soften and loosen up right before your eyes. He may begin smiling and speaking in softer, kinder tones.

TOXIC TYPES IT WORKS BEST FOR

The Angry Bullying Control Freak

Because he is so angry, the bully often needs more love and kindness than anyone else. This toxic personality type often harbors an underlying insecurity and a strong hunger to be loved. In essence, he tries to reject you before you reject him. That is often why he's so controlling. His strong need to be in control is because he's so out of control with regard to his emotions. He feel compelled to control everyone and everything around him. If you understand that about him, you may be surprised to discover he's starved for kindness and affection.

I have seen a bully transform into a little lamb when he is given a smile and a hug and some kind words, despite his loud bullying behavior.

Self-Destructive Gloom-and-Doom Victim

Because the Self-Destructive Gloom-and-Doom Victim is filled with so much self-loathing and self-hate, the Love and Kindness Technique may be exactly what he needs. Sometimes your love and kindness may be the catalyst for a positive change in his life.

Reassuring him, telling him that you love and accept him, and speaking to him in kind and loving terms may be the only way he hears the message that someone actually cares enough about him to help him through his self-destructive tendencies.

8. The Give Him Hell and Yell Technique

HOW IT WORKS

This technique is difficult for most women, who are taught early in life that it's not "ladylike" to be angry or to scream at someone. If you do so, you may be labeled a "bitch." Yet when a man yells at someone who deserves it, he is said to be "tough." In reality, so what if you are called "a bitch" or "a tough broad"? Don't fret about the semantics; what's important is that you're sticking up for yourself. The bottom line is that yelling or giving someone hell may be one of your most effective options for dealing with a Toxic Man because all too often it may be the only way you are actually heard.

In this technique, let it all out at the top of your lungs, contort your face, and even point your finger and throw up your hands in rage. You can roar like a wild tiger to express your anger, but don't hit, scratch, bite, or use any physical violence.

WHY IT WORKS

This method works because it can show the Toxic Man your strength and that you will no longer put up with his horrendous behavior. It shows him that you have boundaries and that you are setting limits. It also give you a sense of strength and empowerment, knowing that you can fight back and won't be bulldozed by anyone.

TOXIC TYPES IT WORKS BEST FOR

The Angry Bullying Control Freak

Often, the bully needs to be bullied. He needs to see that you will not be intimidated by his yelling and screaming and talking over you. Often, your behavior shuts him up because *he* gets intimidated. It is interesting to watch how a control freak can dish it out but can't take it. You may often see him shrink after giving him Hell and Yell.

The Wishy-Washy Spineless Wimp

Sometimes the Wishy-Washy Spineless Wimp needs to be shocked into making a decision, one way or the other. This loud boom, which no doubt upsets him, lets him know that you are not putting up with his indecisiveness and manipulation any longer. With your booming tone, you are letting him know that it's time for him to finally "man up!"

9. The Fantasy Technique

HOW IT WORKS

This technique allows you to release tension by fantasizing what you would like to do to a Toxic Man. While you must *never use violence* or anything that can get you into legal trouble or harm anyone, there is nothing wrong with a little fantasizing of what you would like to do to him.

So feel free to fantasize about doing to the Toxic Man whatever would give you a vicarious thrill, whether it is pushing him into ongoing traffic or doing a Lorena Bobbitt on him. Again, carry it out in your fantasies, not in real life. The consequences are definitely not worth it.

WHY IT WORKS

The Fantasy Technique allows you to release your stress and anger in a nonverbal yet cathartic way. Though you won't follow through on your thoughts, you give yourself a feeling of control over the situation that you may not have in real life.

TOXIC TYPES IT WORKS BEST FOR

The Angry Bullying Control Freak

Since the Angry Bullying Control Freak usually is the toxic type who tends to be an abuser, using the Fantasy technique gives you a lot of relief because you can fantasize giving him a taste of his own medicine.

It works especially well when the Angry Bullying Control Freak is your boss and you can't make waves or you will get fired. Instead of keeping it in and letting him destroy your psyche, fantasize about what would you would like to see happen to him, such as seeing the police arrest him and take him away in handcuffs in front of everyone. The fantasy can be a wonderful vicarious thrill and an instant headache reliever.

Socio-Psychopaths

I know a woman who lost all of her money to a Madoff-type Socio-Psychopath. She lost everything, from her home to her car to her jewelry to her retirement. She was in such despair that she wanted to take a gun and blow his head off. Who could blame her? Thankfully, she didn't do it in real life, but she certainly did it in her fantasy life. Each time she fantasized about it, it gave her some relief.

This technique specifically works for a Socio-Psychopath because you often feel so helpless in his wake. He often does such bad things to you on such an extreme level that it may be impossible to fight back unless you are in a court of law and he is thrown behind bars. The Fantasy Technique allows you the vicarious thrill of getting back at him in your mind without having to deal with the horrible consequences that could happen if you actually did what you fantasized about doing. This technique can be one of the best stress relievers, which can save your sanity.

10. The Unplug Technique
HOW IT WORKS

This technique should be your last resort. It should only be used when you have tried all the other techniques and nothing else works, and you simply can't get through to the man. In using this technique, you need to visualize yourself unplugging from him as you would unplug a lamp from an electric socket. That means you are unplugging yourself from him and all his negative behaviors. You completely let go of him. You no longer care about what he did in the past, what he is doing now, or what he will do in the future. He is now out of your life as if he never existed.

While it may seem harsh, there are times when this is the only option you have. It is not simply walking away and ignoring. It is walking away and consciously letting go of any feelings toward him and never looking back. Most of the time you Unplug forever. But there are times when you may Unplug for a certain length of time only to revisit the situation later on.

This can often be the case where you Unplug because of tough love. For instance, you may unplug until he gets into rehab and changes his toxic self-destructive behavior, or you may unplug until he has gone through a course of therapy. Then you can revisit and see whether things have changed and you can begin a new chapter of your interaction. On the other hand, you may revisit only to discover that he is still the same, if not worse.

There are situations in which you must never look back, such as with a Socio-Psychopath or someone who abuses you. If a man hits you or beats you or hurts your children, run as fast as your feet will carry you.

WHY IT WORKS

With the distance and time you spend away from him during the Unplug Technique, you may get a brand-new perspective that will continue to keep you away or keep you away with certain boundaries, restrictions, conditions, and limitations. Sometimes Unplugging is the only way that you can take a step back and be objective about what's happening and how it's affecting you.

TOXIC TYPES IT WORKS BEST FOR

Socio-Psychopath

This is the only technique that works with the Socio-Psychopath. There is no reasoning with him. There is no loving and kindness. There is nothing other than walking out the door and nailing it shut so he never gets back into your life. He is too dangerous, manipulative, and frightening to deal with. As soon as you discover you are involved with one, in business or personally, leave. Cut your losses and save your psyche and your life.

The Angry Bullying Control Freak

Abusers often fall into this toxic category. If a man verbally abuses you, emotionally abuses you, or mentally abuses you, rest assured physical abuse is next. If you see any of the signs of any of these types of abuse, you must use the Unplug Technique. There is no other choice.

The Self-Destructive Gloom-and-Doom Victim

There are times when you have tried everything and you can no longer sit idly and watch this Toxic Man destroy himself. It may be just too painful to see. That is when the Unplug Technique may be your only choice for the sake of your own survival. Remember that you can never help a Self-Destructive Gloom-and-Doom Victim unless he is also willing to help himself. Otherwise you must Unplug until he takes the steps to get his act together. If he won't do this, you must unplug for good.

The Emotional Refrigerator

You may also need to use this method on the Emotional Refrigerator. No one wants to go through life without love and affection and communication; that is not what life is all about. If you have tried every which way to communicate and it isn't working and your man is still an Emotional Refrigerator, if it proves too frustrating to you, you have to leave.

As I mentioned in the explanation of Emotional Refrigerators, some men who suffer from Asperger's syndrome or another disorder may act that way and be unable to help themselves. Here we are talking about a disability, so I am not asking you to leave that situation at all. I am not talking about those who can't communicate. I am talking about those who are fully capable of communicating but refuse to do so.

Techniques to Break the Cycle of Abuse

All of the Toxic Types may be abusers in their own way. For instance, the usually mild-mannered and cooperative Silent-but-Deadly Erupting Volcano may become verbally and physically abusive after he emotionally explodes. The Emotional Refrigerator may be emotionally abusive by his withholding behavior and lack of verbal and physical affection and communication. The Socio-Psychopath and the Angry Bullying Control Freak often commit verbal, emotional, and physical abuse.

Abuse can happen as soon as you meet someone. Did he make a snide or sarcastic comment to you early on? Did he tell you he was just kidding? Is he rude to you? Has he cut you down or showed signs of verbal aggression toward you? These signals must never be ignored, as they are huge red flags in terms of how the relationship will go.

Does he have a hard touch? Does he get rough with you? Does he ever shove you? Does he give you light slaps or punches on your arm under the guise of being playful or funny? Know that there is nothing funny about this behavior. As soon as you hear someone becoming verbally abusive or rude toward you, or if he play-fights you, you need to put a stop to it immediately. If you don't, it can and often does escalate into something that can become your worst nightmare.

ABUSE AGAINST WOMEN IS ON THE RISE

While both men and women perpetrate domestic violence, studies have shown that men's violence toward women may do more damage than the reverse. According to a 2000 study by the U.S. Justice Department, 64 percent of women who reported being raped, physically assaulted, and/or stalked since age eighteen were victimized by a current or former husband, cohabiting partner, boyfriend, or date. The study also found that women are more likely to be injured than men, with 41 to 59 percent of wives much more likely to be killed by their husbands than the reverse. It also showed that women in general are more likely to be killed by their spouse than by all other types of assailants combined.

In times of economic pressure, the rate of domestic violence toward women rises. Studies show that job insecurity causes symptoms of anxiety and depression in men. This, in turn, may result in more aggression and acts of physical violence. So it is not surprising that the National Domestic Violence Hotline recently released data that suggests a link between financial stress and domestic violence. For victims who called the national hotline during the six-week study, 54 percent reported a change in their household's financial situation in the past year. Similarly, in 2000, the National Institute of Justice revealed that women whose male partners experienced two or more periods of unemployment over the five-year course of the study were three times more likely to be abused.

DON'T IGNORE THE SIGNS

Whenever I have asked an abused woman if, looking back on things, she had seen indications or signals of her mate's abusive behavior early on in their relationship, every woman admitted that she now saw the signs of abuse that she had brushed off or ignored. Some even said that they laughed at it or were flattered by the jealousy and the attention that their man paid to everything they said and did.

You must be vigilant early on in a relationship and *never* ignore any abusive behavior. These toxic behaviors are all warning signs that something worse is coming in the future. At the first sign of abusive behavior, you need to exit. Do not stick around to see what will happen. If you do, you will regret it.

VERBAL ABUSE PHASE, STAGE 1

The Cycle of Abuse starts with verbal abuse—nasty and sarcastic comments followed by "I was only kidding." For instance, it may be something as ordinary as your dropping something on your blouse at dinner. If you don't hear a compassionate comment like "That's too bad" or a helpful comment like "Here's some water to wash it off," but instead hear a nasty and cutting comment like "You're such a slob," followed by "I'm just kidding," note that this is not a very nice person. In fact, it is a toxic and abusive comment. Abusive comments like this not only happen in your personal life, but can occur in your work life as well. Speaking to someone in demanding harsh tones at work is also considered abusive.

As soon as you hear those cutting words coming out of a man's mouth, know that he is making the deepest cut in your psyche and cutting a huge chunk out of your self-esteem. Treat it as though he was making an actual cut in your flesh. Whenever you get the first inkling that any verbal abuse or disrespect is being directed toward you, put a stop to it immediately! You need to never be afraid to speak up for yourself. You can say point-blank, "I don't appreciate being spoken to like that and will not accept it. So please never speak to me that way again." Set your boundary and symbolically draw your line in the sand. That boundary or line must never be crossed under any circumstances. The man must know early on in the relationship that he is not allowed to speak to you in such a manner. There are absolutely no excuses for verbal abuse.

You must never worry that you are hurting his feelings or that he will get mad. If those two thoughts cross your mind, get out of the relationship immediately. You are with a Toxic Man and are headed for a horrific future.

EMOTIONAL ABUSE PHASE

The next step in the Cycle of Abuse is the tears, as you experience constant frustration and sadness. He will take the nastiness of his comments up a notch and really hurt your feelings. He will deprive you or punish you or play head games with you. He will disrespect and abuse you by saying and doing things to bring out your negative emotions that make you feel horrible about yourself. When this happens, you know that you are with a Toxic Man.

VERBAL ABUSE PHASE, STAGE 2: YELLING AND CURSING

This is the stage where you hear the volume of his voice increase and his temper and patience get shorter. His tone may be curt and you may begin to hear obscenities hurled at you as the verbal abuse phase gets even stronger and the abuse more frequent. When this happens, if you don't take charge and put an immediate stop to it, rest assured that things will not only continue, they will get worse. At this point, the Toxic Man needs to be in counseling, with or without you, or take anger management classes.

PHYSICAL PHASE: POINTING TO PUSHING TO PULVERIZING

After the yelling, he may begin finger-pointing, which turns into a little shove, then a little push or a tap, then a light slap, and eventually a full-on physical blow to any part of your body. If you allow it to continue, the violence may become more frequent and more brutal over time. The second anyone lays a hand on you, get out the door. Go to a friend's house, a family member's house, a woman's shelter, or anywhere you can get away from this horrific situation.

According to experts, an abused woman goes back and forth to the abuse an average of seven to ten times. While it is difficult to leave this person for a number of reasons (many of which are mentioned in Chapters 15 in this book), you must do so.

When you are ready and when things get bad enough, there is only one technique to break the Cycle of Abuse, and that is to leave. As uncomfortable and painful as it is, you must go.

CHAPTER 15

Should I Stay or Toss Him to the Curb?

The Hardest Decision

Even though your relationship may be toxic, one of the more difficult decisions you will ever have to make is whether to leave or to stay. No matter what anyone else tells you to do, you must make the ultimate decision. Perhaps the toxic situation with your Toxic Man can eventually work itself out. For example, maybe your man had a fling that you discovered. You may have wanted to leave him because of it, but instead you stayed because you saw how sincerely remorseful he was. You observed significant positive changes in his behavior, with you being his first priority. You may have noticed that he is more communicative and willing to resolve any disputes between the two of you instead of giving you the silent treatment, as he did in the past. The fact that he is willing to go for counseling and willing to learn from his mistakes are also good reasons for you to stay. You see how hard he is trying, and both of you realize how important the marriage is. You realize that the marriage is worth saving only because you are both willing to work at it.

Or perhaps it will never work out. For instance, he may have hit you. Even if he only did it once, it is one time too many for you to ever forgive him and stay with him. If he did it once, chances are he will do it again and again and again. If that's the case, even though you may know deep down that you need to leave, sometimes you can't or won't leave for myriad reasons, which we'll look at shortly.

There are many things that factor into whether you will stay or leave a relationship, and they differ for everyone. With the exception of a man hitting you, there are no set-in-stone reasons for you to make the decision. It all depends on what you can live with. But always remember that whatever you decide, your safety and the safety of your children must always come first in the decision-making process.

DON'T TRY TO PLEASE EVERYONE

No matter what your decision, remember that you can't—and shouldn't try to—please everyone. Conflicting viewpoints are ever-present in these situations, such as: *If I leave him, members of my family may be upset that I'll be raising two kids alone . . . but if I stay, my friends and family will refuse to associate with him.* The most important thing to remember when you've got two sides giving you their opinion is to do what's best for you and your children, if you have any. The rest of the pieces will fall into place, and ultimately you will always know you made the smartest decision you could.

Top Ten Reasons Women Stay with a Toxic Man

After reading so much about Toxic Men, you probably realize that it's very difficult to maintain a relationship with them. But life and matters of the heart are not black-and-white. You likely have a variety of factors that will influence your decision. See if any of the top ten reasons that women stay with Toxic Men are at play in your decision:

1. Your religion forbids it
2. Your cultural background frowns on you leaving
3. You feel you should stay for the sake of the kids
4. You are financially dependent on him
5. You're concerned what friends and family will think if you leave
6. You believe that your Toxic Man needs you and can't be without you
7. You're feeling vulnerable and insecure
8. You're afraid that no one else will want you

9. You feel a sense of hopeless resignation, that it's your fate to stay in this relationship

10. You have a fear of the unknown (if you leave him and must start your life over)

For some women, one or more of these reasons is so strong that she will stay in the relationship no matter what the Toxic Man does to her. If that's the case for you, following is information about how to cope as best as possible with your toxic relationship.

Trying to Turn the Toxic Relationship Around

Coming to a decision to stay with a Toxic Man does not immediately make the relationship any easier. When a relationship is not working, you both know you are no longer getting what you want or need. You can't seem to talk to each other anymore and you don't even want to try. In fact, you would rather spend time communicating with anyone else but your man. You never laugh. You are bored or turned off by his appearance or behavior, especially when you compare him with other men. You detest his toxic behavior to the point that you can barely stand to be in the same room with him.

When you've decided to stay, you, like most nurturing women, can try to change him. But he'll refuses to change, or he'll change for a while then go back to his old ways. At that point, there is so much tension and arguing between you both that you no longer feel good about yourself—your own self-image and self-esteem are suffering. Tears are often a part of your day.

First and foremost, review Chapter 14 and apply one or more of the techniques discussed. You must continue to try different strategies until you find something that works. Your success not only will help relieve your tension, but may elicit more positive behaviors from your partner.

YOU MUST GET OUTSIDE HELP

Even while you employ the ideas in Chapter 14, it's vital to enlist the support of others—professionals who can guide you. Whether it is your clergy or a licensed family and marriage therapist, you must have an objective person on board. It's important that this person have a lot of experience in your problem areas to help you set boundaries, learn better ways to cope, and have more realistic expectations.

There is no way around it; you can't do this all by yourself. You need a third party who has your best interest at heart. Sometimes a third party can be just someone who cares about what happens to you, such as a family member or close friend. But be cautious if choosing a friend or a family member: he or she may have their own agenda or may be biased toward one side or another. If you choose a friend to help serve as a facilitator, make sure that the person cares about both of you and isn't partial to one party or the other. You also need to know that just in case she isn't successful in helping the two of you, it may not only be the end of your relationship with your mate, but it may also be the end of your friendship with the facilitator and her involvement in your life. The old saying "Don't shoot the messenger" may apply here. By her serving as the messenger in trying to relay each party's relevant message to the other, the message may be miscommunicated or get lost in translation and the messenger may ultimately be blamed for it. Since you don't want this to happen, it might be best to stick with an objective third party whom both of you respect.

If You Decide to Leave

While in general I advise clients to do whatever it takes for them to stay together, there are circumstances in which a woman must leave the Toxic Man no matter what. When a man hits you or beats you, you do NOT deserve it, and you MUST leave. If you find yourself thinking, "I must have deserved it," you must change your attitude immediately. Nobody deserves it! No woman, whatever her age or upbringing, must ever think she deserves to be hit or abused.

Though you may have to wrestle with some of the Top Ten reasons women stay with Toxic Men listed on pages 208–209, it's far better to reject these reasons than to continue to subject yourself to someone who is abusing you. The support of a trained professional, friends, or family can help you work through this process. Don't hesitate to ask others to help you, because it may be almost impossible to get away from an abusive partner on your own. Clearly, leaving him will not be easy, especially if you have loved this man and shared a life with him. However, you are literally putting your life at risk if you stay.

Let the Beaters and the Cheaters Go!

There is no question that when a man raises a hand to you, he must be "kicked to the curb," and left there for good. But what about other types of Toxic Men? What about one of the most common Toxic Men—the Cheating Liar? In this day and age, a Toxic Man's cheating can not only have dire consequences on a woman's psyche by causing her emotional distress, but can also jeopardize her physical health to a serious degree.

We no longer live in an age where a mere shot of penicillin can clear up a toxic cheater's indiscretion. If your man lives a double life— engaging in sexual relationships and unprotected sex with other women or in clandestine homosexual relationships with men—carefully weigh whether it is worth the risks to stay in the relationship. Those risks are quite serious: A man who cheats could be subjecting you repeatedly to sexually transmitted diseases, some of which can eventually kill you. HIV and AIDS are life-threatening, as are hepatitis B and C, which can destroy your liver.

Even if your toxic cheater has promised that his indiscretion is over and he will not lie or cheat again, stay vigilant. Watch for body language cues, facial language cues, and vocal and speech cues that indicate deception. Remember, it is essential that you not only pay attention to everything he says, but how he says it. Pay close attention to clues and slip-ups that may indicate that he's fallen back into his toxic ways. Look for sudden changes in his behavior, from his dress and grooming to his schedule. We all want to believe the best about people we love, but though we want to believe that our Toxic Men *can* change, it's sadly not always possible. So keep your eyes and ears open. Don't let yourself be fooled twice.

PART V

Healing from a Toxic Man

CHAPTER 16

Dealing with Pain and Anger

Even if you have physically unplugged from your Toxic Man by ending the relationship, he may still haunt you mentally and emotionally. Just as it took time for him to be out of your physical presence, it will take time for him to be out of your mental and emotional presence. After the initial shock of leaving (or being left), you will go through various stages of the grieving process. Even if it was a toxic relationship, you will be grieving over the loss of what could have been and the loss of your self-esteem. While you may experience initial euphoria once you are away from him, your emotions will feel like a roller-coaster ride as you figure out how to rebuild your life sans Toxic Man.

You will go through the same process that anyone does when she is grieving a death. After all, it *is* a death—a death of a relationship. You will no doubt experience shock, denial, guilt, pain, anger, bargaining, depression, reflection, and loneliness. Then you will make an upward turn, where you actually start the rebuilding process in accepting the reality of what happened.

What no one tells you is that you don't step through these stages in the order I described. One day, you may feel happy because you felt an upward turn. The next day, you may be in shock at the realization at what happened. Then, an hour later, you may be filled with rage, while a minute later you feel guilty and in pain. There are no right or wrong feelings, and no right or wrong sequence they should follow. Whatever you are feeling that particular second is perfectly acceptable.

The unpredictability of your emotions may be frustrating and exhausting, but it's all part of the process of moving on. That is why I can't stress enough that you should reach out to someone who can serve as a support system as you go through this roller-coaster ride of emotions.

Don't Suffer in Silence!

You may feel so embarrassed or ashamed at what happened that you don't want to tell anyone. That is a huge mistake. As I said earlier, you must reach out to someone. Tell a parent, a sibling, a friend, your minister—or even your housekeeper or a stranger you just met on an airplane or in the ladies' room, if you have to. Just tell someone. Suffering in silence can be very bad for your mental health. You must let it out. You need support! Another person's love and support can give you the strength you need to become proactive and make the right change in your life.

SUPPORT MAY NOT COME AS YOU EXPECT IT TO

Even if you are surrounded by a loving family and close friends, you may encounter some unexpected feedback if you ask them for help. You may reach out to someone and be disappointed by his or her reaction to you or your situation. For instance, you may have a great relationship with your sister and think that she would be the only one to completely understand your plight. But you may discover that this may not be the case at all. Instead of being sympathetic to you, she may be highly judgmental and critical of you. Maybe your situation reflects her own insecurities. Maybe she had always looked up to you and seeing you in a vulnerable position is difficult for her to process, so she lashes out.

The reality is that anything can happen when you reach out to people. If you get an unexpected unsympathetic or hostile response from a confidant, tell another person so you can gauge his or her reactions. Continue to reach out to a number of people until you have a number of like-minded people who are in your corner. No one tells you this, but it is important. Remember, the first person you share your story with may not end up helping you. And the friend you thought would be the most supportive may not be who ultimately ends up helping you through your crisis. It may be the person whom you would least expect to understand that is the one who accepts and understands you the most.

Additionally, it is important to know that you may have to reach out to one or more people or to one person for a while and then to someone else a little later in the process. The reason is that some people can handle certain stages of your grieving while others will not be able to tolerate it. Some people are fine when you are in the shock or guilt phase of your grieving, but do not want to be a part of your anger phase. Others won't mind talking about it once or twice but don't want to hear about it every time you speak.

Even though you may be upset at your so-called friends not being there for you when you really need them, you have to realize that most people aren't equipped to help you handle your pain and grief. They may have their own issues going on in their own lives. They may not have the time or energy to devote to you. They may only be able to relate to you when you are happy-go-lucky and not down-and-out. Your pain may stimulate their pain about a similar situation in their lives. They may even think it was all your fault and side with your ex. Understanding this will prevent you from being angry at people for not helping in the way you needed at the time. Don't throw out their friendship because of it. Just know that they were only able to help you according to their own limits and experience. Be grateful and appreciative of what they were able to provide for you and don't let it affect your long-term friendship with them.

MAKE SURE YOUR CONFIDANT CAN KEEP SECRETS

Above all, it's vital that the person or people you ask for help can keep your story confidential. Your supporters should also be able to handle your ups and downs, understand what you are going through, set you in the right direction, and keep a watchful eye on you lest you do something drastic to yourself or others. In particular, you need to know that what you share with a confidant will stay between the two of you and not become fodder for gossip or backstabbing.

For example, let's say that you and your ex were friends with Tim and Sally. After you and your ex break up, you confide in Sally exactly how you feel about what happened. Unfortunately, Sally tells what you revealed to Tim, who now tells the last person you would ever want to know your innermost thoughts: your ex. Besides grieving the loss of your toxic relationship, you will also be grieving the loss of a friend. Avoid this situation by making sure this person has *your* best interests at heart and isn't involved with your ex.

WHERE TO FIND SUPPORT

If you feel that you are having trouble coping, sleeping, eating, and functioning in general, you may want to seek professional help. Whether it is through a licensed therapist, a counselor, a holistic healer, a life coach, or a clergy person, the bottom line is that you need to feel 100 percent comfortable around the person you choose in order to allow him into your life so that he can assist you with your healing process.

Sometimes you will have to go through several professionals to find the right person to help you. This is not a bad thing. Sometimes the person you are seeing may seem right for a while and then later on, you may find that you are not getting anywhere with his help. You may then want to seek help elsewhere. It is all part of the normal healing process. Never feel pressured by anyone to stay and use his services when you do not feel comfortable. Don't worry about hurting his feelings or upsetting him if you leave. Your needs are the most important, not his.

To find a professional to help you, first get recommendations from people you respect and admire. But, once again, remember that if you don't feel comfortable with the person who was recommended, don't hesitate to move on. While that person may have worked for your friend, he may not be suitable for your particular personality or for your needs.

While many mental health professionals may recommend medication for you, if you don't feel comfortable with taking medications, don't feel obligated or pressured to do so. On the other hand, if you are diagnosed with a specific medical condition that may require medication to prevent serious or fatal complications, you must seriously consider taking the medication. If you still don't feel comfortable, then get a second and a third opinion so that you can make an informed decision about what is best for you.

With all that said, many insurance carriers have limited or no mental health coverage. So, for many women, seeing a licensed therapist or psychiatrist is out of the question from a financial perspective. That is why it may be essential to look into other alternatives, such as a women's health clinic or women's shelter. They may provide free or reduced-cost therapy connected with domestic violence matters. The National Domestic Abuse Hotline may be a place to begin, as they are available 24/7 and can direct you. They can be reached at 1-800-799-SAFE (7233).

You could also reach out to your clergy, who are there to help people in emotional need. If you are not religious or if you don't have a spiritual adviser, now may be the time to find one to help you learn more about your spirituality. While it may not be the answer for everyone, it could work for you, so it is probably worth a try. If one spiritual denomination doesn't work for you, you may want to try another until you find what holds promise for you.

One of the best ways to help you heal from a Toxic Man is to attend women's abuse or domestic violence support groups. You can locate ones in your area over the Internet. In these free support groups, you can learn from other women who are either in the same situation or at various stages of the healing process. They completely understand what you have been through and can lend an ear, give advice, and perhaps provide references for legal or housing contacts.

The bottom line is that you *can* find trustworthy, helpful, supportive people to help you. Make an effort to find them. You will be glad you did.

Will the Pain Ever Go Away?

Just as childbirth and passing a kidney stone are immensely painful, so are (a) being in the midst of a relationship with a Toxic Man and (b) healing from that relationship. You may actually experience physical pain—backaches, neckaches, or headaches; loss of energy; tight muscles—in addition to your mental pain—anger, self-doubt, sadness.

Though it may be impossible to imagine when you are in the midst of it, the pain *will* go away eventually. It will certainly take a long time, and you will have ups and downs along the way. The best way to speed up your recovery is to ensure that you're getting help and that you allow yourself to fully experience whatever feelings come along. Don't beat yourself up for any mistakes you've made—they're done and in the past, and no amount of second-guessing will change them. What's most important is that you learn from them and make better decisions in the future. The bottom line is that you are human, and you will make mistakes no matter who you are or how much you know. So you should never beat yourself up. The Toxic Man already did that for you, physically or emotionally, or both. Instead, focus on your positive attributes. Count your blessings and make a gratitude list. On that list, write all of the things for which you are grateful, including the fact that this Toxic Man is no longer in your life. Also list that you are now open for wonderful loving, caring, and genuine people in your life.

If You Want Him Back

It may seem counterintuitive, but some women find themselves wishing they could go back to their Toxic Man. This is very common and a normal part of the grieving process. It is called the "bargaining phase" or "negotiation phase," where you try to convince yourself that what happened with the Toxic Man didn't really happen. You try to make excuses for him as an attempt to understand and process what really happened. You try to convince yourself that maybe he isn't all that toxic or maybe it was your fault that he acted so poorly. You try to a convince yourself that it wasn't that bad or that maybe he needs one more chance and that the next time he will not be so toxic. But this is all illusion. It is your psyche's way of trying to cope with and process the pain of the reality that you have been dealing with a Toxic Man. While your intellect knows that you need to get away from him, your emotions fight for him to stay in your life. This back-and-forth battle between your head and your heart is why so many women end up going back to their abusers. This is so common that studies show that women may go back to their abusers from seven to twelve times before they have had enough and leave for good.

If you have these feelings, visit your support group or counselor, or find one if you haven't done that yet. These people will encourage you to call them before you call him, or not pick up the phone when he calls. They are there to help you stick to your decision and not go back to your toxic tormentor.

Besides leaning on a counselor, a friend, or a support group to hold your hand through these bad times, it is essential that you make a list of all the toxic things he did to you and place that list near every phone in your home. Even tape it to your cell phone. Then when you are tempted to call him and ask him back into your life, you can reread the list. It will refresh your memory and put a stop to your impulse to contact him.

If You Absolutely Hate Him

You may also find yourself feeling the extreme opposite—you may wish either that he had never been born or that he would die. These intense feelings are also a normal part of the healing process. This is when the anger phase sets in. Don't let it scare or upset you. Even though you have been raised and conditioned not to think these hostile thoughts, they are perfectly healthy given the situation you're in.

Of course you are angry at what he did to you, and with anger comes feelings of hate. The more you were in denial of your toxic relationship—if you did not fully face his behavior or abuse—the more anger you will feel toward him postbreakup. The more repressed you were while in the relationship, the more hatred you will experience as your emotions finally come to the surface.

TURNING HATE INTO A POSITIVE THING

Don't be afraid of hating or of saying the word *hate*. Hate is as honest an emotion as love is. They are both extreme emotions. There are degrees to which you love, just as there are degrees to which you hate. Hate can actually be a good thing, if it fuels you into taking positive action. For example, it can fuel you into picking up and slamming down the phone when he calls, or seeking out different routes home from work so you won't see reminders of the relationship that bring him to mind, or getting up and leaving a rude man fifteen minutes into a blind date. It can fuel you into making a better life for yourself, changing your image and your life for the better.

A WOMAN SCORNED—TURNING ANGER OUTWARD

On the other hand, if your hate is not channeled properly into something positive, it can consume you and even destroy you. Hate that is out of control can lead to doing bodily harm to another, which can, in turn, destroy your life. Today's news has plenty of stories of women who may have been abused and wronged and let loose a torrent of rage against their perpetrators. There are stories of women who have defaced property, or run over, shot, stabbed, and even cut off the penises of their cheating mates.

When a relationship with a Toxic Man ends, for some women the pain is so excruciating that they turn the pain outward in the form of violent anger, committing bodily harm to their ex or his property—for example, throwing black paint on the wall of his office, burning his clothes, or hacking into his Facebook account. Just remember that there are legal consequences for these acts. Turning your hurt outward to temporarily address your anger will only make matters worse for you in the end. When all that damage is done, the relationship still happened. No amount of lashing out will change that.

What can also bring forth a woman's rage is when someone does something to her child, as in the case of Ellie Nesler, who walked into a courtroom, pulled a gun from her purse, and point-blank shot in the head the man who molested her then eleven-year-old son. Even though most women would want to do this, they weigh the consequences of their actions and are deterred by the possibility of serving prison time. (Nesler went to prison for her act.) Therefore, they would only carry out this act in their fantasies as we discussed earlier in the book. While you can fantasize about actions like this, *never act on your thoughts*.

INFLICTING BODILY HARM ON YOURSELF: TURNING ANGER INWARD

Just as aiming your anger at the perpetrator is not an option, neither is directing the anger inward. You may feel such guilt, pain, or shame that you turn your rage toward yourself. You may start drinking, overeating, or having rampant unprotected sex, just to dull the pain. But the only person you hurt in the long run is you. You may become so angry at yourself that you completely shut down and refuse to ever allow any man into your life again—or worse, begin to hate men in general.

Often, you are not only grieving for the relationship that ended, you are grieving for yourself and all that went wrong in your life. When that happens, it is easy to spiral deeper and deeper into the depths of depression and hopelessness. When you think thoughts such as "What am I living for?" "Who cares about me, anyway?" or "No one would miss me if I was gone," it's time to seek professional help immediately. You could be a few steps away from committing the ultimate act of self-destruction—suicide. That is yet another reason for you to reach out for support during these emotionally fragile times.

Under any circumstances, *suicide is not the answer*! If you have thoughts of it, tell someone immediately and seek help from a qualified board-certified psychiatrist—a medical doctor (MD). He or she will know exactly what to do. You may need medication, hospitalization, or both, and this is the only mental health professional who can make sure that these needs are addressed. Even if you feel friendless or alone, there are people out there who can support and help you. There are people out there who do care about you, even if you don't know who they are. You will find tremendous support at a women's abuse or domestic violence group or on a suicide hotline. Look up suicide prevention hotlines online or call 411 and have them connect you to one in your area.

If you have gone so far that you have a plan of action developed in your mind as to how you will commit suicide, call 911 immediately and tell the operator that you are thinking of killing yourself and to send help. You can also go to the nearest hospital's emergency room and let them know. They should have mental heath professionals on staff who can give you the help you need. The bottom line is to get immediate help because this is an emergency! Even if you are feeling at your lowest, know that this feeling will pass. As painful as it is, it is temporary. That is why you must do everything possible to help yourself through this crisis period. Eat or do whatever gives you an immediate fix until you can get through this low point. Then be sure to get professional help so this situation does not occur again.

Emotional Pain Relievers That Really Work

Instead of wallowing in your pity and pain, here are some things you can do to relieve your pain. Even though some may seem unconventional or odd at first, they do work. They are designed especially to get you through those very low points.

EAT, DRINK, AND BE MERRY

As it says in the King James version of the Bible, Ecclesiastes VIII:15 "To eat, and to drink, and to be merry." During a difficult crisis period, I say why not eat and drink to your heart's content? I am only talking about your crisis period, not about doing it for the rest of your life. You don't need to add additional health and emotional problems to your life that come with being excessively overweight.

I am also not talking about drinking if you are an alcoholic or have allergies to alcohol. If you have alcohol issues, skip the drink part and just eat and be merry.

Eating and drinking can help you heal because they are self-soothing devices. Eating your favorite comfort foods when you really need to be comforted can make you feel immediate relief.

FIND SOME LOVING

During a crisis period, you need to be held tenderly and hugged and caressed and treated kindly. If you can find a lover for some (safe and protected) "Band-Aid therapy," I say why not? The one thing you don't want to do is to jump into another heavy-duty relationship. The chances that your lover will be nothing more than a rebound relationship is pretty high. So spare yourself the additional heartbreak. Know that your intention is a temporary romance, because expecting anything more from another person is lying to yourself and setting yourself up for disaster.

No matter if it is with an old boyfriend or a "friend with benefits," being made love to can be very healing at this point because it not only releases sexual tension, it confirms that your body does indeed work on a physical level. On an emotional level, it confirms that there is someone else out there with whom you can make love—your Toxic Man isn't the only man out there. But tread carefully in this area. Be aware that if you make love with someone else before you have processed your feelings about your Toxic Man, you may be setting yourself up for another emotional disaster. You run the risk of projecting the emotions you had with your toxic lover on to your new lover. So be careful emotionally and physically. Use caution, and above all, protect yourself from STDs.

GET A MASSAGE

You need physical contact to heal; that's why having sex has the potential to be a good emotional healer. However, there are other ways to get a similar feeling, such as getting a massage. Yes, they can be expensive, but forgo that new pair of shoes or going out to an expensive restaurant and instead spend that money on a weekly massage. You will be glad you did.

There is something about being naked and being massaged with a slick oil film all over your body that makes you feel vulnerable enough to release all the excess tension in your body that comes from emotional pain. The massage table can be the safest place for you to really sob your guts out and get to the core of your heartache. Being pampered will also give you something to which you can look forward each week. If you simply can't afford it, try the barter system. If you have no skill to barter, offer to clean the masseuse's house, babysit her children, wash her car, or do her grocery shopping.

Another way to feel a healing touch is to visit a spa where they bathe and scrub you. Some large cities have Korean or Japanese bathhouses. Being washed and having your dead skin scrubbed off is not only incredibly healing, it is symbolic. Having your dead skin scrubbed off, leaving you with a fresh new lawyer of healthy, glowing skin, is symbolic for starting a fresh new life. It is kind of like a snake shedding his old skin.

SURROUND YOURSELF WITH BRIGHT COLORS

There is a whole psychology of color. Studies show that your emotional state can be affected by certain colors. Even if you feel as if a bulldozer has just run over you, when you get dressed in the morning, choose clothing with the brightest hues. Any bright color will work, from turquoise to fuchsia to red to emerald green to royal blue. You need energy and these colors stimulate your visual systems, which, in turn, stimulate the pleasure centers in your brain and therefore make you feel happier. So stay away from pastels and subtle tones and black at this time.

The same holds true for your home. Now is the time to go to one of those discount stores and pick up some colorful throw rugs and matching pillows, candles, and glassware. If you can't afford to move or renovate your home, simply changing a small aspect of your living environment with a quick, colorful pick-me-up will do the trick. Go from room to room and figure out things you can change that won't cost you a fortune. Maybe it's getting a fire-engine-red throw rug with matching pillows, new colorful paintings or artwork for your walls, a bright happy yellow-and-blue print tablecloth with matching napkins, or a new purple wall clock. These simple items can change the entire miserable mood of your past living situation. It will often feel like a new home with new energy, symbolically starting a new, bright, and happy beginning.

Besides the redecorating, take this opportunity to declutter. Clean out your closets, attic, and basement. Don't be afraid to comb every nook and cranny of your home and either put away, donate, or sell on eBay anything that gives your heart or tummy a negative twinge. That cashmere sweater and all the jewelry he gave you can be sold for good money online or at a pawn shop. Those cute stuffed animals he gave you while dating can be donated to a children's hospital. All his now-meaningless love letters can be thrown away. Throwing out items that bring back sad memories gives you more space (both physically and emotionally) to create new happy memories.

GOSSIP, CELEBRITY, AND FASHION MAGAZINES ARE GREAT COMFORTERS

There is nothing like reading the tabloids to discover that a famous star who was just dumped by her boyfriend feels as crappy as you feel. It's called *schadenfreude*, a term that describes how you relish others' misery because it helps you feel better about your own misery. When you see a photo of that celebrity (whose body you always envied) and discover that she has packed on the pounds just like you, suddenly you don't feel so bad.

If you aren't interested in celebrities, try a fashion magazine. There is something about turning those slick, shiny pages of a magazine like *Cosmopolitan* (where I have a monthly body language column called "The Real Story") that makes you feel good. Looking at the photos and fashions of the models can be inspirational and motivating. Seeing a model with a cool haircut may be a catalyst for you to get a new hairstyle, which may elicit more attention from others and make you feel better about yourself. Seeing a certain accessory, shoe, or style on a model can be the channel that allows you to update your look, which also allows you to feel more self-confident and more hip.

DO ARTY AND CRAFTY THINGS WITH YOUR HANDS

One of the most popular healing activities offered to those dealing with mental disorders, especially in institutional settings, is arts and crafts therapy. The old jokes about patients doing basket weaving are actually true. Doing something with your hands and focusing on other aspects of your brain can be calming and very healing. The creative process and the resulting items that you created are very therapeutic for your self-esteem.

Whether it is jewelry making, knitting, painting, sculpting, gardening, weaving (cloth, baskets, or hair), or manicuring someone's hands or feet, the bottom line is to do something with your hands. It will refocus your brain and calm your mind.

HANG OUT WITH LIVING THINGS

While pulling your down-filled covers over your head and lying in your safe, soft cuddly bed all day and night may be comforting for a while, in the long run it can get old. It can also become habit-forming, turning you into a hermit. Getting out is important because you'll see that other people still live and function on this planet. Many of them have been through terrible breakups and moved on. Force yourself to do errands such as grocery shopping, picking up things from the drugstore, or running to the post office. Though you can do almost anything online these days, go back to old-fashioned shopping for now. Other activities count, too: doctor, dentist, therapist, massage, manicurist, women's support group, and lunch and dinner appointments with friends and family.

If you don't have any friends or family to speak of at the moment, now is your chance to make some new friends, who may even turn out to be like family. Join a local group that aligns with your hobbies—for example, a ballroom dancing class, a quilting group, a book club, or a religious study class. That way, you'll know that these people at least share some common interests with you. If you are too shy to jump into a group setting, try to make some connections online. Make Facebook or MySpace friends. Go into support group chat rooms for the recently separated or divorced. You can even go on a dating site and meet new men that way. But again, be sure that you do not start a full-blown relationship. Simply use the casual dates as a way to get you out of your comfy bed and back into life.

Now is also a good time to contact people from your past. Even if it has been three decades, contact people who were once in your life. Perhaps you lost friends while you were married to a Toxic Man who controlled who you associated with. Start fresh with them by briefly summarizing where you are now and suggesting a lunch date to catch up. Your reaching out will invite them to rejoin your life again. Also, find out when your next class reunions are. Even if you didn't know many people in high school or college, going to a reunion decades later affords you the perfect opportunity to make new friends with people who shared your same educational experience.

If you are very lonely, you may want to think about volunteering with kids, being a Big Sister, or even being a foster parent to a child who needs a loving home. Also, consider adopting a puppy or a kitten. There are many pets in animal shelters who crave a loving home. You may be saving each other's life—literally, in at least one case. It may also be a good time to nurture some plants and start a garden. As you plant seeds, you are symbolically planting the new seeds of your own life, and you can watch both your garden and your life grow in a new direction.

DO SOMETHING YOU NEVER DID BEFORE AND ALWAYS WANTED TO DO

Now that you have shed the old, as part of your healing process you have to try the new. Try foods you never ate before or never thought you could eat. If you ever wondered what crocodile or kangaroo tastes like, now may be your time to try it. If that's not for you, what about getting an international cookbook and systematically sampling all the cuisines of the world in your own home? It can also be an excuse to invite new friends over to sample your cooking.

You can also learn things you always wanted to learn. Even if money is tight, perhaps you can take some free or reasonably priced classes that offer you a way to learn unique skills—from handwriting analysis to rock climbing to salsa dancing. Doing so also puts you in an environment to meet new people and open new dating possibilities.

One of the things the loss of any relationship brings into focus is that nothing lasts forever. Use that realization to seize the day. Life is fleeting; don't let it pass you by. Have you ever wanted to travel the world? Do it now! You will be surprised at how inexpensive it can be. These days there are many cheap travel deals and vacation packages you can take to travel and explore the world—or the next state over if that's more your speed. Where there is a will, there is a way! You can be more frugal in your spending on food, dining, clothes, and entertainment so you will have more money set aside for travel. Selling what you no longer need or use on eBay can help you channel money into your travel fund. Seeing new places, involving yourself in other cultures, and broadening your horizons can give you a richer and brighter perspective of life.

LAUGH EVERY DAY

Psychologist Norman Cousins was the first to popularize the medical benefits of laughter. He apparently was able to slow the progress of his own fatal illness by watching comedies and laughing every day. His scientific research actually proved that "laughter is the best medicine." He used the same techniques with his own patients and found that they were less depressed and were able to recover from many of their ailments.

Institute weekend-long comedy-watching marathons, or spend ninety minutes a day watching a comedy to help keep depression away. Sitcoms, cable's Comedy Central, or comics and humor books can also work wonders in terms of making you feel good. Even though you may not feel like smiling, studies show that if you place your lips in a smiling position you will begin to feel happier. So force yourself to smile at least five times a day and you should begin to notice an improvement in your moods.

KEEP A JOURNAL OF EVENTS, YOUR REACTIONS, AND YOUR FEELINGS

When you find yourself feeling particularly horrible on certain days, try writing down your most intimate thoughts and feelings. Express your raw emotions; hold nothing back. Write what you see, think, and experience. Doing this is a great exercise because in the future, you can look back to see just how far you have come emotionally. You will have a record of the emotional depths of the hell you once lived through. Write things down as soon as they happen and as soon as you experience them so the emotions are fresh in your mind. This journal can also serve you well during the legal process should you go through a divorce, as you can document your emotional turmoil. It helps you see everything more clearly and in perspective as you see the facts in black and white.

You can write by hand, type on a laptop or PDA, or audio-record yourself or make a video diary of what you are experiencing and feeling as it happens. Just know that in some states it is against the law to record a person without their legal permission, so keep this a private project and do not record anyone else.

Your journal can also come in handy if you want to try your hand at screenwriting. Hollywood is always looking for a good script. Wouldn't it be something if your personal experience with your Toxic Man became the basis of a romantic comedy, a mystery, or an intense drama? The beauty of your taking charge and writing it down is that you can make it turn out however you want. You can make it a happy ending using your wishful-thinking fantasies, or you can call upon your more violent fantasies and kill him off with brutal bloody murder. The choice of how your script ends is unlimited, and is yours.

COUNT YOUR BLESSINGS

There is a wonderful song by the a capella group The Nylons called "Count Your Blessings." There is so much truth in the lyrics. Whenever you are feeling low, write a list of what *is* working in your life and for what you are grateful. Determine your top three things and etch them into your psyche. Think about them each day when you get up in the morning, in the middle of the day, and before you go to sleep at night. Say a prayer of gratitude for those three things. People who do this focus more on the good than on the bad in life and are happier.

"LOVE ABSOLUTELY EVERYTHING THAT EVER HAPPENS IN YOUR LIFE"

If you go online and look up famous quotations on the subject of life, you will see quotes from great writers and thinkers such as Maya Angelou, Kahlil Gibran, Benjamin Disraeli, Mahatma Gandhi, and Winston Churchill. Along with those I add a quote from my late and great friend, Dr. Paul Cantalupo, MD: *"Love absolutely everything that ever happens in your life."* What Paul meant was that we should love both the good things and the bad things that happen to us, because they are all a part of our lives.

You may think that this advice sounds strange. After all, how can you love a terrible experience with an awful person? It's not easy to see at first, but even though dealing with a Toxic Man was a bad thing that happened to you, it was still a part of your life. Perhaps as a result of your relationship with a Toxic Man, you learned some lessons that allowed you to become an even better, more compassionate, aware, or understanding person. Perhaps your bad experience will help you to inspire others so they won't make the same mistakes. Perhaps as a result of dealing with a Toxic Man, you completely changed your life around for the better. Perhaps you became more successful, made more money, and found the right man for you (a man who wasn't toxic!). Perhaps the experience allowed you to tap into other areas of your life, from developing your creativity to uncovering your hidden talents.

The bottom line is that your black cloud may also have a silver lining that balances your life. It is ying to your yang, black to your white, up to your down, and good to your bad. The more distance you have from the relationship and the farther you have come in healing and moving on, the more clearly you will see these silver linings.

CHAPTER 17

Forgiveness and Living Happily Ever After

It's Okay to Never Forgive!

You may feel that certain things your Toxic Man did are simply unforgivable. I personally believe that it is okay to not forgive some things. I believe it is perfectly healthy to have feelings of hatred—the opposite extreme of love. I feel that it is normal to not forgive certain people under certain circumstances. So never feel guilty if you cannot find it in your heart to forgive some Toxic Man who has ruined your life.

Though some people disagree with this idea, I also believe that hating and living with the anger toward a toxic person is a good thing, as it serves as an emotional reminder and prevents you from allowing what happened to you to ever happen to you again. Feeling anger toward another person should never be considered a bad thing. In fact, suppressing your anger and living in denial that you are not angry is a very bad thing. You must be able to experience the wide gamut of emotions in order to be real and genuine with your feelings. You must never ignore or deny any of your emotions— especially your anger. Doing so may cause your anger to eventually explode with greater, possibly inappropriate, intensity. It can also cause your anger to implode, which can cause a multitude of physical and emotional ailments.

If You Choose to Forgive

On the other hand, if you feel that you have to forgive your Toxic Man in order to heal and move on, I am all for that. But never forget what happened to you. Some people may remember the terrible domestic violence that occurred to Connie Culp, whose husband, Thomas, shot her in the face. Though she was critically injured and completely disfigured, she told the press she forgave him and still loved him despite his horrific actions. If Connie Culp needs to forgive Thomas in order to heal, that is her choice, but she must never forget that Thomas blew her face off. Since certain things that people do are truly heinous, perhaps the only way you may be able to forgive is to look to your religious or spiritual beliefs. If this is an option for you and it helps you cope, you may find that forgiving the Toxic Man who caused you such pain may provide a great deal of emotional comfort for you throughout your life.

However, it may not work for everyone. Even though you may consider yourself a spiritual or religious person and try to forgive your perpetrator, you still may experience anger toward him, if not hatred. Never feel guilty about experiencing those particular thoughts and feelings. Know that this is normal and that you should never deny or suppress your true feelings.

Forgiving Yourself

Whether or not you choose to forgive the Toxic Man, there is one person whom you absolutely must forgive in order to heal: YOU.

Many women never speak to others about the mistakes they made or the choices they wish they had made differently. They are understandably too embarrassed and humiliated. They would never dream of telling anyone, for example, that they were involved in an abusive relationship and stayed in it for years. Whether or not you admit what happened to someone else (and again, it's best for your emotional health if you *do* tell someone), you must admit to yourself that it happened. Before you can heal, you must reject any denial and excuse-making. Even if you think what happened was all your fault, partly your fault, or not at all your fault, the bottom line is that you have to forgive yourself for whatever happened.

It takes a long time to forgive yourself, especially if you are a person who tends to be hard on yourself. You probably can't believe that you, of all people, got involved with a Toxic Man. Maybe you saw the signs, yet you remained in the relationship in order to fix him or change him. As silly as it sounds, one of the ways to forgive yourself is to look at yourself in the mirror and speak to yourself out loud just as you would speak to your best friend. As you have that "conversation," tell yourself what you honestly think you did wrong in the relationship—whether it was trying to change him, staying in the toxic relationship for too long, putting up with his abuse, being too nice or too lenient, taking him for granted, allowing him to take you for granted, allowing your kids to see his abusive behavior, or giving him too many chances. Say whatever you feel may be your fault or contribution. Then say your full name and say "I love you (full name) and I forgive you (full name)." Now smile and give yourself a forgiveness kiss in the mirror. You may even want to put on some lipstick when you kiss the mirror and leave your lip print on the mirror as a reminder of self-love and self-forgiveness.

If you falter and find yourself feeling self-doubt again, repeat the exercise in a different mirror, once again leaving your lip-printed kiss as a reminder of self-love and self-forgiveness. In fact, you may want to say "I love and forgive you" before you leave a lipstick-kiss print on each and every one of your mirrors, including your small compact and makeup mirrors. This way whenever you look at yourself you will be reminded of forgiveness and self-love.

WRITE, AUDIOTAPE, OR VIDEOTAPE A LOVE LETTER OF FORGIVENESS TO YOURSELF

One way to help forgive yourself is to write yourself a letter of love and forgiveness, which you must keep forever. Because you may still be experiencing myriad emotions, from anger to hatred toward the Toxic Man, it is essential that you get all your true feelings out by writing, audiotaping, or videotaping how this Toxic Man impacted your life both positively and negatively. Look at the entire picture of your relationship. Discuss the history of your relationship and pinpoint when things broke down. Talk about how you felt about what happened. Then discuss what he did to create the break in the relationship and what your role was. Now, forgive yourself for whatever you feel you did or don't do. Tell yourself that it is time to move on and that a wonderful new life is awaiting you. List all the great things about yourself. The more times you tell yourself that you are loved by you and that you forgive yourself, the greater the chances that you will begin to embrace this concept and believe it.

Cautions to Consider While You Rebuild Yourself

Though creating a new, healthy life for yourself is very exciting, it's important to keep a few things in mind as you move forward.

1. DON'T MAKE MAJOR DECISIONS UNTIL YOU ARE EMOTIONALLY HEALTHY

When you are depressed or have gone through significant trauma, you often don't always think rationally because of all the chemical changes going on in your brain. That is why it is essential to postpone making major decisions—from getting plastic surgery to selling your home—until you are a little more emotionally stable.

When you are in the grieving and healing process, your decision-making skills may not be as clear as they usually are. Again, here's where a therapist, friends, family, or support group can lend a hand. You need to run your ideas and decisions past a group of people you can trust. While the ultimate decision is yours, your support group can help guide you in the right direction so that your mistakes are kept at a minimum.

If some time has passed and you have done the four things from the "Strategies to Help Rebuild Your Life" list on page 240, you may be ready to take the next step and make some bigger changes in your life.

2. ACCEPT THAT REBUILDING WILL TAKE AWHILE

It's not uncommon for you to feel as though your life is moving in slow motion. Don't be worried if it takes you a long time to rebuild.

You will do what you have to do whenever you are ready. While some people can bounce back and rebuild in matters of weeks, others may take a decade before they are truly ready to rebuild. So don't put a time limit on rebuilding your life.

For those of you who are go-getters, don't be upset if business or social ventures come to a complete stop in your life You may not have the emotional energy to pursue them or you may be conflicted about what to do next. There is nothing you can do to force the healing process to speed up. There is a natural course of events that you must go through. No one knows how long that will take. Know that it will take time to renew yourself, so try your best to be patient and go with the flow.

3. REBUILD YOUR ESTEEM – WITH BOUNDARIES!

Now that you have changed or are in the process of changing what you never liked about yourself, you are on your way to having a much healthier self-esteem. Only when your self-esteem is high can you completely heal yourself from the trauma of having dealt with a Toxic Man.

Self-esteem gives you the added confidence that you will never repeat the same mistakes. Because you are in charge of your life, you have choices. Next time around, you will make sure that the only man allowed to enter your life is a Nontoxic Man. For this to happen, immediately after meeting someone with whom you may become involved you must set boundaries and be alert to the first signals of toxicity. While regaining your self-esteem is itself a great accomplishment, be sure that it is accompanied by protective actions that prevent future Toxic Men from infiltrating your life.

That means that the first time you hear critical words followed by "I was just kidding," you'll know that this is a man to whom you should say "No thank you." While no one is perfect, there is a Nontoxic Man out there who is perfect for you. That is why you have to say no to the ones who are wrong for you.

4. HANDLE REJECTION WITH GRACE AND APLOMB

As you navigate new environments and engage in new situations, you will eventually be more proactive when it comes to meeting men. You will no longer have to wait for a man's attention or his courage to ask you out. It's up to you to make the first move.

If your move is rebuffed, however, you need to "woman up" and not turn the rejection inward, thinking something is wrong with you. He could be rejecting you because you are not his imprinted type. He could be rejecting you for countless reasons that have nothing to do with you. That is why you need to look at rejection in a different way than you did in the past. A man's "rejection" is your "protection" against the wrong man, who may not fully appreciate you. Thus, think of his rejection of you as a blessing in disguise.

Strategies to Help Rebuild Your Life

Only when you are emotionally and mentally ready can any rebuilding take place. Nietzsche's philosophy of "that which doesn't kill you makes you stronger" is very true. Here are a few ways to begin rebuilding your life to become an even better version of yourself.

LOOK FOR PATTERNS IN YOUR PAST

See a clear picture of what happened, not only in your most recent relationships, but also in every relationship you have ever had. Return to the list you made in Chapter 3 of all the Toxic Men you have ever associated with. Look for patterns in your choices of men and examine your own roles in the various relationships. What toxic behaviors did you allow to take place? What would you do now, in retrospect, to make sure this never happens again?

SEND A LETTER OR E-MAIL TO THE TOXIC MAN

While most experts say to write a letter but throw it away or do not to send it, I strongly believe in sending your letter to the Toxic Man. But if you have been in a physically abusive relationship where you must not have any contact with the Toxic Man, write the letter but DO NOT send it. In that case, you must not have contact with his man under any circumstances. Write everything you always wanted to say to him and then let your words and your emotional connection to him go forever. Feel free to let all your emotions out and even name-call if it makes you feel better. Make sure that what you write can't be construed as threatening bodily harm, threatening his life in any way, or threatening to harm his loved ones or his property. Otherwise, you may put yourself in legal jeopardy. Also remember that he may share this letter with others, so you may want to consider that when you write him.

The following is an example of a letter you may wish to write him to let him know that he is out of your life forever.

Dear X:

The thought of you absolutely repulses me. I cannot believe that I have wasted so much of my time with you. I went into our relationship with an open heart and so much trust and respect for you. Today I am feeling the exact opposite. I have absolutely no respect or love for you. How you treated me throughout our relationship was unconscionable! You were verbally and emotionally abusive.

I thought that with all the love I gave you, you would change your ways, but I was sadly mistaken. Your selfishness will never endear you to anyone in the long run. If you keep going on the path you are on, there is no doubt that you will die a miserable and lonely man. It is clearly in your best interest to seek professional help. But knowing how stubborn and arrogant you are, I am sure that you will never even entertain the thought.

I come away from our relationship having learned a great deal. I learned that I am worth so much more and that I will never under any circumstances allow any man to treat me as poorly as you have treated me.

I completely release you from my life forever. I want nothing to do with you. Never call me, e-mail me, or contact me under any circumstances. I have no interest in you and even less interest in how you are doing. The door is nailed shut with regard to you, so never dare attempt to reopen it! I have moved on and will NEVER look back.

Don't expect any reaction or response to your letter. You are not doing it to manipulate or to find out how he will react or think. Instead, this is your final statement. It is your conclusion to that toxic chapter in your life. It is the written closure that will help cement your healing process and allow you to build a new future.

If you have had problems severing contact in the past and/or accepting the change in the relationship, please contact a professional to help you. In your particular case, they may advise you not to write the letter so be sure to seek their counsel ahead of time.

GET TO KNOW YOU!

If you've been in a particularly long or emotionally involved relationship with a Toxic Man, you may have almost lost your identity because of his behavior and treatment of you. For example, if your Toxic Man was controlling or abusive, he may have altered your sense of self and your knowledge of what you like and dislike to the point that you barely know yourself anymore. If you have had little choice about how to live your life, you may find now that you don't know where to start! Fill out the following "Dr. Glass Getting to Know Me Survey," which I designed in order to help you learn about your likes, dislikes, feelings, and visions for the future. This survey will help you realize the importance of understanding everything about yourself—both good and bad—before you can even think of engaging in a serious relationship with any new man.

Just fill in the blanks with the first thought that comes into your mind. Don't edit it or answer what you think would sound good to others (and certainly not what the Toxic Man would want you to say!). Instead answer truthfully and from your heart.

DR. GLASS GETTING TO KNOW ME SURVEY

My name is _____.

If I could change my name, it would be _____.

I am _____ years of age_____.

I wish I were _____ years of age. _____.

I live in _____.

I'd rather live in _____.

My family is _____.

The perfect family is _____.

I make my living _____.

I would rather make my living _____.

My friends are _____.

I wish my friends were _____.

Socially, I _____.

Socially, I would rather _____.

The qualities I value most are _____.

The people I always seem to meet are _____.

I would like to meet _____.

I love people who are _____.

I can't stand people who are _____.

My favorite person in the world is _____.

I love to dress _____.

I hate to dress _____.

I love going to _____.

I dread going to _____.

Financially, I am _____.

Financially, I'd rather be _____.

Physically, I am _____.

Physically, I'd rather be _____.

I would love to _____.

What makes me laugh is _____.

What makes me cry is _____.

It saddens me that _____.

I am disgusted by _____.

I could scream when _____.

My biggest pet peeve is _____.

What embarrasses me is _____.

I am suspicious of _____.

I am exhausted by _____.

I feel guilty about _____.

What makes me angry is _____.

I get frustrated by _____.

I am most confident when _____.

I am hurt by_____.

What makes me laugh is _____.

I am frightened about _____.

I am cautious about _____.

I am jealous of _____.

I am shocked by _____.

I am worried and anxious about _____.

I am bored by _____.

I am hopeful about _____.

I am overwhelmed by _____.

I am ashamed by _____.

I am attracted to _____.

I am surprised by _____.

I am confident about _____.

I am furious about _____.

When I feel rejected, I _____.

When I feel accepted, I _____.

I never worry about _____.

I usually put off _____.

I am excited about _____.

I am turned off by _____.

Others see me as _____.

I see me as _____.

When I meet a man I like, I _____.

When I meet a man I don't like, I _____.

My ideal mate is _____.

In one week, I want to _____.

In one month, I want to _____.

In one year, I want to _____.

In five years, I want to _____.

I would be the happiest person if _____.

The Good News about Me

My greatest accomplishment is _____.

My best asset is _____.

I'm proud of myself when I _____.

My greatest talent is _____.

The best thing about my appearance is _____.

The best thing about my personality is _____.

The best thing about my character is _____.

My fondest childhood memory is _____.

My fondest teen memory is _____.

My fondest memories are _____.

Three positive adjectives to describe me are _____.

I feel attractive when _____.

I feel sexy when _____.

I feel powerful when _____.

The best things I do for myself are _____.

The best people I surround myself with are _____.

The Not-So-Good News about Me

My biggest regret is _____.

The thing I dislike most about me is _____.

The thing I dislike most about my personality is _____.

The thing people "call me on" the most is _____.

The worst thing I do to myself is _____.

The worst thing I did as a child is _____.

The worst thing I did as a teen was _____.

The worst thing I've done as an adult is _____.

I'm most insecure about _____.

Three negative things that describe me are _____.

Look at all of your answers. This is who you are. Accept it! Love it! It's YOU! Only when you accept all of you—warts and all—can you even think about sharing yourself with someone else.

This list can help you determine the path your life should take. It allows you to see in black and white exactly what you want to do and gives you the opportunity to think about how to get there. For example, if you want a different career, the fact that you have now expressed it in writing allows you to take a closer look at what you really want and perhaps even make a move to enroll in classes during the next semester. If you wrote that you like being around funny guys, it is a visual reminder that if you want to be happy and laugh a lot more, you should only date guys who make you laugh. Knowing this, you might even attend more comedy-oriented events and spend your entertainment dollars on tickets to comedy clubs.

CREATE THE IDEAL YOU

Now that you know who you are, the final step in the rebuilding process involves creating the ideal you. It is the time to stop pleasing everyone else and start pleasing *yourself*, perhaps for the very first time. This involves listing everything you don't like about yourself and making significant changes. Whether it is your weight, your hair, your teeth, your education, your job, lack of friends, lack of travel, the way your home looks, or where you live—change what you don't like. This is the step where you stop being a victim and do whatever it takes to make those positive changes without any excuses. List everything you have ever wanted to do and DO IT NOW!

Because you now know what to listen to and what to look for, if you choose to venture into the dating scene, the remarriage scene, or the happily single scene, you will jump back into a happy and positive life with your eyes wide open.

CHAPTER 18

There *Are* Nontoxic Men Out There!

The True Gentleman

My dear, beloved brother Manny tragically died in my arms in a medical malpractice situation where he was intubated improperly by a resident physician who was only a doctor for seven months. At the hospital, I went through his belongings and found a card in his wallet. I took it out and read it:

The True Gentleman is the man whose conduct proceeds from good will and an acute sense of propriety, and whose self-control is equal to all emergencies; who does not make the poor man conscious of his poverty, the obscure man of his obscurity, or any man of his inferiority or deformity; who is himself humbled if necessity compels him to humble another; who does not flatter wealth, cringe before power, or boast of his own possessions or achievements; who speaks with frankness but always with sincerity and sympathy; whose deed follows his word; who thinks of the rights and feelings of others, rather than his own; and who appears well in any company, a man with whom honor is sacred and virtue safe.

I discovered later that this card, which Manny always carried with him, was the creed of his fraternity, Sigma Alpha Epsilon, and was written in 1899 by John Walter Wayland. Manny lived by this creed, as he was a true gentleman in every sense of the word.

You Can Find a Good Man!

I wish I had a dollar for every time I heard a woman say "A good man is hard to find" or ask "Where are all the good men?" The answer is simple: They are everywhere. The truth is that they are easy to find, if you know what to look for. When you stop looking for Prince Charming to rescue you in your personal or business life and look instead for the "Real Deal" kind of man, you will be surprised at how many wonderful men come your way.

After reading this book, you now have a keen sense of awareness concerning Toxic Men. Therefore, it is easier to quickly spot them and weed them out of your life. Conversely, you will know whom to encourage into your life, so that you can enjoy fruitful business and personal relationships.

"Am I Around a Wonderful Man?" Questionnaire

Still, some of you may still be shaky when it comes to having the confidence to choose the right man. Since your track record may not have been great in the past, you wonder if you will slip up and make those mistakes again. The reality is that you may make a mistake again. You may unintentionally let a Toxic Man get past the gates of your life. But now, he won't get far or stay for long. Unlike before, as soon as you recognize his toxic ways, he will be out the door.

Here are some yes and no questions to ask yourself when you meet a new man in your life for business or personal reasons. The answers will help you determine if this is indeed someone whose presence you should encourage.

1. Do you feel energized after being around him?
2. Do you feel that there is mutual like and respect?
3. Do you feel confident, worthy, attractive, and/or intelligent when you are around him?
4. Do you feel as if something is missing when you are away from him?
5. Do you feel safe and secure around him?

6. Do you feel like laughing or smiling whenever you think of him?
7. Does he sing your praises around others?
8. Do you feel that he "has your back," is supportive and loyal?
9. Do you feel more motivated around him?
10. Does he bring out your best behavior?
11. Are your affections or feelings reciprocated?
12. Do you feel and act naturally and comfortably around him?
13. Does he seem genuinely concerned about you?
14. Does he unselfishly go out of his way for you or try to please you?
15. Is he generous with his time, feelings, and efforts?
16. Does he speak to you in kind or loving tones?
17. Is it difficult for you to leave his presence when you are with him?
18. Do you share a lot of interests and activities?

If you answered Yes to most of these questions, you are no doubt with a wonderful man. If you answered Yes to half of the questions, you may want to dig a little deeper into his personality and see if you're just still getting to know him, or if he may harbor a few toxic tendencies. If you have answered Yes to only a few or none of the questions, it's likely that this man doesn't have enough of the qualities you are looking for, and is probably not a good match for you.

Which Type of Man Is Specifically Wonderful for You?

Just as you figured out in Chapter 3 which men were specifically toxic to you and to which you were specifically allergic, you can now figure out which men are specifically wonderful for you. Throughout your life, you have most likely met wonderful men who have brought out the best traits in you. You felt great when you were around them; they had traits you admired and respected. Whether it was a professional relationship or a personal one, you two were a good match.

Here is what to do to find wonderful men now:

1. Make a list of ten men whom you have admired and respected throughout the years. The man can be a parent, relative, teacher, boss, coach, clergyman, or even someone in the public eye whom you may not know personally but still admire. Reflect on every man who has been in your life from childhood to the present.
2. Next to their names, list three or more positive traits that best describe them. If you get stuck, here are a list of words to help.

LIST OF POSITIVE DESCRIPTIONS OF A NONTOXIC MAN

accepting	bright
accommodating	brilliant
accomplished	bubbly
active	calculated risk–taker
admits mistakes	calm
affectionate	calming
alert	carefree
amazing	caring
ambitious	centered
animated	cerebral
appreciative	charismatic
approachable	charming
articulate	chatty
assertive	childlike
athletic	classy
aware	clean
backbone	clearheaded
balanced	clever
bold	committed
brave	communicative
brazen	compassionate

concerned

confident

connected

conscious

consistent

cool

creative

credible

curious

daring

decent

decisive

deep

definite

deliberate

delightful

demonstrative

discerning

diverse

down-to-earth

easygoing

easy to talk to

eccentric

eclectic

educated

educating

elegant

emotive

emotional

emotionally open

energetic

enlightening

enterprising

enthusiastic

entrepreneurial

even-tempered

evolved

exciting

expressive

fair

family-oriented

fastidious

fatherly

fearless

flexible

focused

forceful when needed

forthright

friendly

fun-loving

funny

generous

genuine

giving

goal-oriented

good listener

good-natured

good values

gracious

grateful

gregarious

guiltless

gutsy

happy

hardworking

healthy

helpful

hilarious

hip

honest

honorable

hot

humble

humorous

imaginative

independent

industrious

inner-directed

inner strength

innocent

innovative

integrity

intellectual

interested

in-the-moment

intuitive

joker

joyful

kind

knowledgeable

larger than life

laughing

law-abiding

leader

learns from mistakes

levelheaded

likes himself in a healthy way

limitless

listener

lively

loving

loyal

manly

masculine

mature

moral

motivating

neat

noncompetitive

nonviolent

not adversarial

not aggressive

not blaming

not complaining

not defensive

not guilt-ridden

not invasive

not jealous

not judgmental

not self-destructive

not self-righteous

not threatening

not troubled

not victim-like

nurturing

old-fashioned values

open

open-hearted

open-minded

optimistic

orderly

organized

outgoing

passionate

patient

people person

perceptive

personable

philanthropic

playful

positive

powerful

predictable

proactive

prominent

protective

proud

provocative

punctual

quick-witted

quiet

rational

real

realistic

reasonable

religious

remorseful

reputable

respectable

respectful

responsible

secure

self-assured

selfless

self-motivated

sense of humor

sensitive

sensual

sensuous

serious

sexual

sharp

simple

smart

sober

social

socially aware

soft

soft-spoken

spiritual

stimulating	unselfish
straightforward	unsuspicious
strong	upbeat
studious	up-front
successful	verbal
sweet	vulnerable
talented	warm
talkative	well-groomed
tenacious	well-mannered
tender	well-read
thoughtful	well-rounded
trusting	well-spoken
trustworthy	willing
truthful	winner
unafraid	wise
unashamed	witty
uncomplicated	worthy
uncritical	zealous
understanding	Zen-like
uninhibited	zest for life
unpretentious	

3. Now, compare the men's positive traits. You will find that the men share many similar traits. This tells you that these traits are what you should look for in the men you welcome into your business and personal life. It gives you a guideline of what qualities are most important to you. You need not accept any man into your inner sphere unless he has these positive qualities.

When you are with men whose traits suit you best, you will discover that the relationships are easier. They flow because you tend to understand one another much better. There is no hidden agenda, so things are more up-front. Relationships tend to be more equal because there is more respect and more open communication.

Profile of the Nontoxic Man—"The Real Deal"

Just as there are profiles for specific types of Toxic Men, there is also a profile for a Nontoxic Wonderful Man, also known as "The Real Deal." Just as most Toxic Types do not exhibit each and every characteristic, neither will most Real Deals have every single one of these traits. The key is that you get an overall picture of a man who is caring, thoughtful, and sincere.

SPEECH PATTERNS

The Real Deal is verbally generous. He speaks with politeness and is respectful. He has manners and speaks with terms of endearment. He usually thinks before he speaks so he doesn't make many faux pas. He is loyal and conscientious about what he says. He is sincere in his compliments. He speaks positively, seeing the brighter side of life and the glass as being half full.

The Real Dealers of the world are people of their word. They say what they mean and mean what they say. They are not hypocrites and they do not lie or exaggerate. They realize that they are responsible for the consequences of their actions. Therefore, they speak and act accordingly. They accept people as they are and don't judge them, and are friendly and open to almost everyone. They are interested in others, as opposed to being worried about being interesting *to* others. They focus outwardly, not inwardly. They use the term "you" a lot, and not "I." They will use "I" and relate to themselves only if what they are talking about includes or can be related back to you. For instance, you may say, "I like to go to the zoo." He may say, "Me too. I love the San Diego Zoo Wild Animal Park. Have you been there?" If you say no, he might say, "I can tell that you would love it. You would be so impressed with how the animals roam free."

A Real Dealer would never talk "at" you. Instead, he would talk "with" you. He shares information and makes sure that there is always give-and-take during the conversation. He communicates in a down-to-earth, sincere manner, often possesses a good sense of humor and a light-heartedness, and would never use sarcasm or make cutting comments to you. He does not get laughs at the expense of others.

Real Dealers are excellent listeners and tend to draw out the best in others. You really feel comfortable around them and find yourself opening up to them, telling them things you normally wouldn't tell others because they aren't judgmental. They give you their opinions without being offensive. Finally, they share openly about themselves and aren't afraid to let you know who they are.

VOICE

A Real Dealer uses a wide range of emotion in his tone when he speaks to you. He speaks in a manner that reflects emotion appropriate to the situation that is being discussed. Whether he is happy, upset, afraid, or unsure, you will clearly hear it in the variety of inflections in his vocal tones. This makes him interesting to listen to. You are never bored. He is present and aware of the flow of the conversation. The pitch of his voice and volume of his voice vary, depending on what he is discussing. He is not afraid to let out his true emotions through his voice. He doesn't hold back vocally.

He has clear and intelligible articulation and his voice is rich and resonant. It sparkles with the enthusiasm that he usually has toward life and the people around him. He has a robust quality in the way he speaks that makes people want to listen and take notice. His voice gives you a sense of comfort as you continue to feel at ease around him when he speaks. If you are in distress, he often gives you great comfort just through the sound of his voice. Its sincere sound makes you feel as though he really cares about you.

BODY LANGUAGE

Real Dealers are loose and fluid in their body movements. They are open and inviting and make others around them feel very comfortable.

They often lean in toward the person with whom they are speaking. They tend to nod their heads in order to provide the other person with the encouragement he or she needs to continue speaking. In essence, they indicate their interest by getting close enough to the person without invading his or her space.

Even though they are relaxed and comfortable, they have a posture that exudes confidence with head erect, shoulders back, and a straight spine. Their gestures are grand and large and they enjoy hugging and touching. They often speak using their arms as a form of expression to show interest and to express important points they wish to make. When they gesture, the palms of their hands are often exposed with their fingers extended. This indicates that they are open and have nothing to hide. Their legs are apart when they sit or they cross their legs at the knee for comfort. This is further indication of their openness. Their feet are planted on the ground and there is no shuffling or shaking of the feet or crossing or uncrossing of the legs when they speak to you (which could indicate nervousness or deception). Their toes face in the direction of the person with whom they are speaking, which reflects that they are being sincere with that person and genuinely like him or her.

FACIAL EXPRESSION

The Real Deal has excellent eye and face contact. He has a steady gaze that does not make you feel uncomfortable or uneasy. If he really likes you, he will spend more time looking into your eyes, but won't stare at you or make you feel uncomfortable. He looks right at you when he speaks and does not break his gaze. That means he does not look around the room. You are the focus of his attention and he makes you feel as though you are the most important person in the world. He gives you his 100 percent undivided attention.

His facial expression is normally relaxed and open, which indicates how receptive he is toward you. He has fluid facial movements, a relaxed jaw, and a sincere slight smile when listening and speaking. When he is really excited or happy, his face reflects this. He gives you a genuine smile where the corners of his mouth are turned up and there is wrinkling around the corners of his eyes. This communicates genuine joy and happiness.

He reflect a facial expression that matches his verbal expression. If he is speaking about something that makes him happy, you will see that expression in his face just as you will see sadness when he speaks of something sad. He is not afraid to wear his expressions on his sleeve. If he likes you, his pupils will enlarge and light up and the sides of his nose will flare out a bit—and, of course, he will smile a lot.

Be Realistic but Have High Standards!

While no man is perfect, there are of course a set of standards that he must meet in order to be considered Nontoxic. Even if a man has a few flaws, it doesn't necessarily mean that he is a Toxic Man. In fact, as mentioned before, what one woman may consider as being toxic may not be toxic to you based on your own personality makeup. The bottom line is to be open-minded so that you don't close off all your possibilities.

Conclusion

When you follow the guidelines in this book, you can quickly and easily identify any man who may be toxic to you. Now you will know with whom you are dealing well before you get involved with him. This will spare you the grief of going through a miserable relationship, because you can now discern exactly the type of man who is toxic to you. If you are not sure, ask yourself the questions in Chapter 1. If he comes up short, you can no longer make excuses. You know that your limbic system, located deep in your brain, is giving you a message. Whether you call it instinct, a sixth sense, or a gut feeling—listen to it! Always remember that the body does not lie! Neither does the voice or their speech pattern. The truth eventually reveals itself.

Another important point: You have choices. You are no longer a victim and no longer have to suffer in silence. You can choose to leave any relationship, and indeed you *must* immediately leave one where you are being abused. On the other hand, if you have made the decision to stay, you can use the techniques in Chapter 14 to make the most of the relationship. Some strategies will work better than others, depending on the type of Toxic Man. If one of the techniques doesn't work, try another one. Keep trying until you find one that does work, so that your life can become more bearable. If nothing works, re-evaluate your decision as to whether to stay or leave. If you decide to leave, then you must incorporate the final option—the "unplug technique," where you not only unplug physically from the Toxic Man but unplug mentally and emotionally as well.

The healing process does not happen overnight. But know that there is indeed a light at the end of the tunnel. Even though you think this is the darkest point in your life, when you do come out of the pain and the anguish, you will be a wiser and stronger person. Your life will be richer and have even more meaning, because you have taken action and put yourself in charge of it!

Index

About the Author

Dr. Lillian Glass, "The First Lady of Communication," is a well-respected and foremost authority in the field of communication. As an internationally renowned body language expert and media personality, she shares her unique perspective about newsmakers and current events throughout the media. She is a regular commentator on *The Nancy Grace Show*; the body language expert for *Dancing with the Stars, Entertainment Tonight, Swift Justice, Dr. Phil,* and *The Insider*; and the resident therapist on *Chelsea Lately*. She often appears on MSNBC as well as numerous other television shows. She has a monthly body language column in *Cosmopolitan* magazine called "The Real Story." Dr. Glass also writes a blog for *Psychology Today*, as well as her own Dr. Lillian Glass Body Language Blog. Her comments can be read regularly in magazines and newspapers worldwide.

In the entertainment field, Dr. Glass has worked with many of Hollywood's award-winning actors, helping them achieve certain specific body language and voice patterns for their outstanding performances. In the legal field, Dr. Glass is a qualified expert witness in both state and federal court in the area of vocal forensics and behavioral analysis. She is also serves as a jury consultant.

Dr. Glass has authored fourteen books, including her original bestseller *Toxic People: 10 Ways of Dealing with People Who Make Your Life Miserable* and a book on body language, *I Know What You're Thinking: Using the Four Codes of Reading People to Improve Your Life,* available in every language throughout the world.

Based in Beverly Hills, California, Dr. Glass considers herself a citizen of the world. She lectures internationally with her mission always in mind—"Global Peace Through Communication." Visit her website, *www.drlillianglass.com*, where you can purchase her products and services and read her daily blog about the body language of newsmakers and what they are really saying between the headlines.

Getting Where Women Really Belong

- Trying to lose the losers you've been dating?
- Striving to find the time to be a doting mother, dedicated employee, and still be a hot piece of you-know-what in the bedroom?
- Been in a comfortable relationship that's becoming, well, too comfortable?

Don't despair! Visit the Jane on Top blog—your new source for information (and commiseration) on all things relationships, sex, and the juggling act that is being a modern gal.